PUBLISHER COMMENTARY

I0011560

Weapon Systems Software Management Guidebook 15 August 2008

This guidebook is specifically directed at Computer Systems and Software (CS&S) associated with weapon systems. Lack of software management guidance has been identified as a major concern for Air Force organizations involved in the acquisition and sustainment of software-intensive weapon systems.

A recent GAO report presented the argument that Department of Defense (DOD) weapons systems under development are riddled with vulnerabilities that make them an easy target for adversaries trying to control them or disrupt their functions.

This guidebook addresses these known issues and sets top level Air Force expectations for the development, acquisition, management and sustainment of weapon systems software and software embedded in Air Force systems, so that software-related problems that are now too typical can be understood and avoided in the future. The principles and techniques in this guidebook will generally apply to all software domains, but the targeted domains include aeronautical, electronics, weapons, and space systems. The intended audience includes Project Officers, systems/software engineers, and other engineers that have a software acquisition element in their project.

Why buy a book you can download for free? We print this book so you don't have to.

First you gotta find a good clean (legible) copy and make sure it's the latest version (not always easy). Some documents found on the web are missing some pages or the image quality is so poor, they are difficult to read. We look over each document carefully and replace poor quality images by going back to the original source document. We proof each document to make sure it's all there – including all changes. If you find a good copy, you could print it using a network printer you share with 100 other people (typically its either out of paper or toner). If it's just a 10-page document, no problem, but if it's 250-pages, you will need to punch 3 holes in all those pages and put it in a 3-ring binder. Takes at least an hour.

It's much more cost-effective to just order the latest version from www.Amazon.com

This material is published by 4th Watch Publishing Co. We publish tightly-bound, full-size books at 8 ½ by 11 inches, with large text and glossy covers. 4th Watch Publishing Co. is a Service Disabled Veteran Owned Small Business (SDVOSB). Please visit www.usgovpub.com.

Other books available on www.Amazon.com:

GAO Weapon Systems Cybersecurity (GAO-19-128)

GAO Green Book (GAO-14-704G) - Standards for Internal Control in the Federal Government

GAO Yellow Book (GAO-17-313SP) - Government Auditing Standards

GAO Financial Audit Manual (GAO-18-601G)

GAO Technology Readiness Assessment Guide (GAO-16-410G)

GAO Cost Estimating and Assessment Guide (GAO-09-3SP)

DoD 7000.14 - Financial Management Regulation

Defense Acquisition Guidebook (Chapters 1 - 10)

Federal Acquisition Regulation - Complete

Defense Federal Acquisition Regulation – Complete

OMB No. A-123 - Management's Responsibility for Enterprise Risk Management and Internal Control

OMB A-130 & Federal Information Security Modernization Act (FISMA)

Federal Information System Controls Audit Manual (FISCAM)

United States Air Force

Weapon Systems Software Management Guidebook

Secretary of the Air Force for Acquisition
(SAF/AQ)

15 August 2008

Version 1 (Abridged)

NOTICE AND SIGNATURE PAGE

Copies of this guidebook may be obtained at:
AF Portal Science, Technology & Engineering Functional Home Page:
<u>Air Force Weapon Systems Software Management Guidebook, August 2008</u>

SAF Acquisition Center of Excellence Website:
<u>Air Force Weapon Systems Software Management Guidebook, August 2008</u>

THIS GUIDEBOOK IS HEREBY APPROVED FOR PUBLICATION.

_____   _15 AUG 2008_____
TERRY J. JAGGERS, SES   Date
Deputy Assistant Secretary
(Science, Technology and Engineering)

NOTE: This abridged version is published with all links to secure (https) web sites removed.

Table of Contents

1 Introduction

Lack of software management guidance has been identified as a major concern for Air Force organizations involved in the acquisition and sustainment of software-intensive weapon systems. Over the past ten to fifteen years, virtually all previously existing software-related Air Force policy, guidance, and training has been rescinded or eliminated. This has happened even as the software contribution to overall weapon system capability continues to increase, and almost all software intensive system development efforts are challenged to satisfy their cost, schedule, and performance baselines. Results of numerous independent reviews have shown that problems encountered on past programs are being repeated on current programs.

Section 804, "Improvement of Software Acquisition Processes," of Public Law 107-314, *Bob Stump National Defense Authorization Act for Fiscal Year 2003*, placed a new emphasis on software acquisition process improvement, focused on acquisition planning, requirements development and management, project management and oversight, and risk management. Furthermore, the Act requires metrics for performance measurement and process improvement, a process to ensure acquisition personnel have appropriate experience or training, and a process to ensure adherence to acquisition processes and requirements.

This guidebook addresses these known issues and sets top level Air Force expectations for the development, acquisition, management and sustainment of weapon systems software and software embedded in Air Force systems, so that software-related problems that are now too typical can be understood and avoided in the future. The principles and techniques in this guidebook will generally apply to all software domains, but the targeted domains include aeronautical, electronics, weapons, and space systems. The intended audience includes Project Officers, systems/software engineers, and other engineers that have a software acquisition element in their project. Software engineering is an integral part of system acquisition and systems engineering (SE), and the guidance offered herein is intended to fit within and support current management and systems engineering approaches in Air Force systems and acquisition programs.

This document, when combined with related Air Force policy, existing technical references, and training, is intended to help acquisition and sustainment organizations more rapidly and more predictably deliver capability by learning from the past, establishing realistic and executable plans, applying systems engineering processes in a disciplined manner, and engineering systems right the first time. The purpose of this guidebook is to provide concise guidance for organizations that acquire or sustain systems that involve significant development, integration or modifications to their embedded software. It should not be used as policy or referenced in contracts. Rather, it provides an overview of the activities necessary to have a successful system/software acquisition.

The term Software Intensive Systems (SIS) is used frequently in this guidebook, as well as throughout numerous Air Force and Department of Defense (DoD) acquisition policy and guidance documents and Joint Chief of Staff publications. A consensus definition of this term is provided for this guidebook:

    a. A Software Intensive System (SIS) is:

        (1) A system in which the majority of functionality is achieved through software, or where mission success depends directly on the correct operation of software; or

(2) A system in which software is a significant factor in system development cost, system development risk, or system development time.

This guidebook is specifically directed at Computer Systems and Software (CS&S) associated with weapon systems. Such CS&S applications are also known as embedded systems, defined as computer systems and software that are a part of a larger system and satisfies some of the requirements of that larger system. Examples include CS&S in an aircraft, missile, satellite, command and control center, training systems, or weapons. The guidance herein is also applicable to the design, development, coding, integration, and testing of firmware. Finally, while this guidebook is organized to align with new start programs, most of the guidance herein can be easily adapted and applied to legacy programs that are implementing new capability blocks/increments.

While this guidebook is applicable to all Air Force embedded systems, it is recognized that there are differences in acquisition policy and guidance between the space and non-space domains. A goal for the next version of this guidebook is to better harmonize the approaches between these two domains where possible, and provide more specific domain guidance where necessary.

Please forward recommendations for changes or improvements to this document to:
Mike Nicol, ASC/EN, (Michael.Nicol@wpafb.af.mil),
Ernie Gonzalez, SAF/AQRE, (Ernesto.Gonzalez@pentagon.af.mil), or
Lt Col Scott Conner, SAF/USAP (scott.conner@pentagon.af.mil).

2   Background

2.1   Why We Have "Software" Problems

Many reasons have been documented to explain why software so often becomes an issue for weapon system acquisition programs. Here are a few of the most frequent based on Air Force experience.

2.1.1   Planning Based on Unrealistic Expectations

Weapon system acquisition programs routinely aim to develop and deliver unprecedented warfighting capability. This unprecedented capability is often realized by developing complex, SIS or integrating existing systems and subsystems with other equally complex systems in new ways. Since acquisition programs are planned and estimated when only top-level performance requirements are available, it is extremely difficult to develop high confidence estimates and align expectations early in the program life cycle. Such early estimates are relatively subjective, involve numerous assumptions, and are almost always optimistic since the engineering activities that result in a complete understanding of the work to be accomplished have not been completed. This complete understanding typically does not mature until well into the design phase, and when it does, it usually confirms that initial estimates were optimistic, key assumptions (such as significant reuse) cannot be achieved, more work than planned needs to be done, and the amount of software that has to be developed and/or integrated is growing. Reuse is a particular problem that suffers not only from excessive optimism about reuse efficiencies, but also from the often unplanned effort required to integrate reused code, to accommodate the adverse impacts of unused or dead code in reused packages, and to address vulnerability assessments, platform selection, platform integration, user interface, and related information assurance concerns. Furthermore, any change to requirements (such as increased scope) must result in a change to the software estimate. Experience shows that even these early optimistic estimates frequently exceed the available program budget and schedule. This can lead to pressure to adjust the estimates to fit the funding profile or the desired schedule. In the face of such pressure, it is very difficult for estimators, technical staff, or program managers (PM) to defend their estimates.

2.1.2   Desired Software Performance is a Moving Target

Most acquisition professionals would agree that a complete, stable, and detailed set of requirements is a pre-requisite for high confidence estimates and successful software development. However, for weapon systems, early requirements are often incomplete or abstract enough so as to require significant interpretation. It is difficult for a potential developer to bid realistically to such requirements, since the software-related work that must be accomplished is so difficult to accurately quantify. The impact of this situation is magnified when the subject program is large, complex, or unprecedented, and the situation worsens when requirements changes are introduced after work on a particular software build or increment has progressed into design or a later phase. There are no free changes for software, and this is true even when *removing* capability, and any change to requirements must be accompanied by appropriate adjustments to budget and schedule.

Frederick P. Brooks, author of *The Mythical Man-Month*, states in the article "Essence and Accidents of Software Engineering," (*IEEE Computer*, April 1987): "The hardest single part of building a software system is deciding precisely what to build. No other part of the conceptual work is as difficult as establishing the detailed technical requirements, including all the interfaces to people, to machines, and to other software systems. No other part of the work so cripples the resulting system if done wrong. No other part is more difficult to rectify later."

2.1.3   *Software Risks not Thoroughly Identified and Effectively Managed*

It is tempting to assume that by applying good management techniques, problems that plagued past embedded system software development efforts can be avoided. All too often this proves untrue. Certainly there is a spectrum of outcomes between failure and success, and legacy programs that have developed, integrated, and delivered some capabilities have climbed the learning curve. Such organizations typically become more predictable over time. But it is a mistake to assume away common risks, especially for new programs working toward the first delivery of a product. As the <u>Air Force Software Technology Support Center (STSC)</u> has noted, "Risk factors are always present that can negatively impact the development process, and if neglected, can tumble you unwittingly into program failure. To counteract these forces, you must actively assess, control, and reduce software risk on a routine basis."

Certain software risks exist on every embedded system software development effort. One example is the basic growth in the amount of software that must be developed as the job is better understood. Another example is erosion of planned software reuse, which again typically results in growth in the amount of software to be developed, or rework to integrate some other solution. Yet another frequent example is failure to produce software at the rate anticipated (e.g., lines of code developed per day) and used in program estimates. Such risks need to be addressed in every program's risk management approach, but there are many more software-related risks that must also be identified and managed. More information on risk is provided in section 3.3 of this guidebook "Management of Software Related Risks."

As Tim Lister (well known software consultant and principal of the Atlantic Systems Guild) states: "Risk management is not risk avoidance when it comes to software projects. All the software projects with high value and low risks were done years ago. Almost by the simple definition of your mission, software efforts at your organization are going to be high risk. Raise expectations and you raise risk. It is just that simple."

2.1.4   *Software Development Teams not Adequately Staffed, Stable, or Capable*

The developers of large, new start embedded systems routinely have problems meeting initial staffing requirements due to the sheer numbers of personnel that must be identified, brought on board, and cleared into the program. Once past that challenge, there is the problem of staff turnover. It's not uncommon for weapon system software development staff to turn over 10% or more per year, and this contributes to a constant learning curve that can have a serious impact to productivity. Finally, there is significant individual variation in productivity. Steve McConnell, Founder, CEO, and Chief Software Engineer, of Construx Software, notes that researchers have found variations ranging from 10x to 28x in coding speed, debugging speed, defect-finding speed, percentage of defects found, bad-fix injection rate, design quality, and amount of code generated from a design. Considering these factors, it is easy to see how even those programs fortunate enough to start out with the "A-team" can experience significant variation in their overall productivity during the development life-cycle.

2.1.5   *Effective Software Processes not Established or Consistently Applied*

The ability to successfully develop large, complex, unprecedented software systems in part depends upon having effective processes institutionalized and implemented with discipline. This includes acquisition processes for the Government and development processes for the contractors or organic organizations that actually develop the software. For new programs, the adequacy of development processes is normally evaluated to some extent in source selection, and the proposed program is examined to see that utilization of the processes fits within the program budget and schedule. Acquisition organizations (those Air Force organizations that acquire and/or contract for sustainment of systems) must resist the temptation to gain false savings by negotiating out the systems and software engineering processes. Attention to detail is required throughout this complex, multi-step process to ensure the developer team commits contractually to using the critical processes, and that the overall program budget and schedule is adequate to allow the processes to be continuously and effectively applied. Abandoning established, disciplined processes when difficulties arise usually leads to more problems. Process discipline should be viewed as an enabler to predictability, since it reduces variation by individuals or groups.

2.1.6   Ineffective Systems Engineering Interface to the Software Development Process

Although many program failures are labeled as software failures, the root problem often traces to a lack of systems engineering at the system level. By definition, embedded software in weapon systems does not function alone; rather software functions within a complex system of hardware that is performing a complex mission. Disconnects between the systems engineering process and software can manifest in countless forms. Beyond the details of input/output (I/O) interfaces with hardware, problems often occur when inadequate requirements deconstruction from the system or subsystem result in unknown requirements to software developers.

It is important for acquirers to be aware that many hardware issues will have a ripple effect on software development and may have the potential to be solved through modified software. The iterative application of the systems engineering process provides an integrated framework within which refinements made in one area may impact other areas and change their results. This evolution continues until a balanced system is achieved. This can only work when all elements of the system, including software, are part of the process. Like the function of embedded software in a weapon system, systems engineering activities serve little purpose if they are performed in isolation. Continuous communication between systems engineers, domain experts and software developers is a must to ensure the thread of systems engineering passes through software.

2.1.7   Lack of Effective Management and Insight into Software Development

It is difficult to manage software with the same rigor as other products, since the relationship of a "completed" requirements document, a top level design, etc. to a completed working software component is not obvious. It is typical for software status to appear normal or on-schedule for long periods of time and then change overnight as an important milestone approaches. The late notice may be due to inadequate progress metrics, misinterpretation of what the metrics portrayed, or an unanticipated failure. The bottom line is that the search for truly predictive software metrics has been elusive, and achieving dependable insight into software status requires continuous attention, even when the development appears to be going well.

Unfortunately, many of the issues noted above are all too familiar in weapon system programs. Dr. Barry Boehm, developer of the Constructive Cost Model (COCOMO) for software estimating, and author of a number of software development textbooks and papers, states that "Poor management can increase software costs more rapidly than any other factor." The good news is, as weapon system acquirers, Air Force program office personnel can have a significant influence on how software for weapon systems is managed. The guidance that follows is intended to directly address these critical issues.

2.2 Air Force Software Policy

In order to meet the requirements of Section 804 and improve the efficiency and effectiveness of Air Force acquisition processes and software management, SAF/AQ/US Memorandum 04A-003, "Revitalizing the Software Aspects of Systems Engineering," (20 September 2004), originally identified ten software focus areas that programs must address.

This policy has subsequently been incorporated into AFI 63-101, "Operations of Capabilities Based Acquisition System," (July 2005), and AFI 63-1201, "Life Cycle Systems Engineering," Attachment 8, (July 2007).

The ten focus areas and their associated tasks mandate that software engineering practitioners and managers must:

a. Estimate software development and integration at a high level (80-90%) of confidence.

b. Ensure program baselines support the disciplined application of mature systems/software engineering processes, are compatible with the overall program's Expectation Management Agreement (EMA), and are supported by the program's budget.

c. Manage computer systems and software specific risks as an integral part of the program risk management process.

d. Identify the software-related strengths, weaknesses, experience, process capability, development capacity, and past performance for all developer team members with significant software development responsibilities.

e. Ensure the developer team establishes and applies effective software development processes.

f. Ensure the program office establishes and applies effective acquisition processes, is adequately staffed, and supports application of effective processes by the developer team.

g. Collect and analyze Earned Value Management (EVM) data at the software level.

h. Employ a core set of basic software metrics.

i. Plan and develop life cycle software support capabilities and support operations.

j. Support the transfer of lessons learned to future programs by providing feedback to center level Acquisition Center of Excellence (ACE) and other affected organizations.

AFI 63-1201 requires programs to address these software focus areas, as a minimum, throughout the life cycle, beginning with pre-Milestone A/Key Decision Point A activities. AFI 63-101 requires programs to incorporate the focus areas as appropriate in the program System Engineering Plan (SEP), Integrated Program Summary (IPS), or acquisition plans. Program Executive Officer (PEO) may tailor the implementation of these focus areas as required, with appropriate supporting rationale, but the Service Acquisition Executive (SAE) should be notified of all tailoring. Tailoring includes developing and implementing additional procedures and/or reducing already stated procedures, where appropriate.

The focus areas described in AFI 63-1201 cover the entire acquisition life cycle. Additionally, this instruction discusses how other processes must include software as a consideration. For example, Human Systems Integration (HSI) must be addressed throughout the life cycle, and must be consistently integrated into systems engineering implementation to balance total system performance (hardware, software, and human).

AFI 63-101 addresses the acquisition planning, requirements development and management, project management and oversight, and risk management process improvement requirements cited in Section 804. PEOs are required to determine how to implement the remaining Section 804 requirements (metrics for performance measurement and continual process improvement, appropriate experience or training for acquisition personnel, and implementing and adhering to established processes and requirements) within their portfolios.

SEP guidance (OSD Systems Engineering Plan (SEP) Preparation Guide, October 18, 2007, Version 2.0 and AFI 63-1201) requires software planning to be addressed in the systems engineering processes. The SEP must remain consistent with the Life Cycle Management Plan (LCMP) which documents the integrated acquisition and sustainment strategy for the life of the system, which, as described in AFI 63-101, includes software considerations. AFI 63-101 also discusses software as an element of specific functions in the acquisition process.

2.3 Mapping Policy to this Guidebook

TABLE 1 maps the requirements of the policy memo and AFI 63-1201 to section 3, Software Acquisition Process Guidance, and the appendices, of this guidebook. Primary focus area guidance is designated with a **bold "X"**; additional guidebook guidance related to the focus area is designated with a **bold "o"**.

TABLE 1. Mapping Policy to Guidance.

Guidebook Sections	Software Focus Area Reference # (See list below in TABLE 2)									
	1	2	3	4	5	6	7	8	9	10
3.1 Software Aspects of Acquisition Program Planning	o	X	o	o	o	X	o	o	X	
3.2 Estimating Software Size, Effort, and Schedule	X	X	X	X	o	X				
3.3 Management of Software Related Risks	o	o	X	o		X				
3.4 Source Selection Considerations	o	X	o	X	X	X		o		
3.5 Applying Earned Value Management to Software		o			o	X	X			
3.6 Establishing and Managing Software Requirements	o	X	o			o				
3.7 Acquisition Insight and Involvement					o	X	o	X		
3.8 Safety Critical Systems			o	o	X	o				
3.9 Non-Developmental Software			o			o			o	
3.10 Software Assurance and Anti-Tamper Protection			o			o				
3.11 Configuration Management		o			o	X				
3.12 Life Cycle Support			o		o	o			X	
3.13 Lessons Learned			o							X
Appendix A: Software in the Integrated Master Plan					X					
Appendix B: Software Content for the SOO/SOW			o	X		o				
Appendix C: Software Content for RFP Section L	o	o	o	X		o				
Appendix D: Software Content for RFP Section M	o	o	o	X		o				
Appendix E: Software Contracting Considerations			o	X		o				
Appendix F: CS&S Criteria for Technical Reviews				o	X	o				
Appendix G: Process Considerations for Safety Critical Systems					X					
Appendix H: Air Force Core Software Metrics								X		
Appendix I: Software Development Plan					X					
Appendix J: Glossary of Supporting Information										

NOTE: Key: **X** – Primary Guidance
           o – Supplemental Guidance

TABLE 2. Software Focus Areas.

Focus Area	
Ref. #	**Title**
1	**High Confidence Estimates**
2	**Realistic Program Baselines**
3	**Risk Management**
4	**Capable Developer**
5	**Developer Processes**
6	**Program Office Processes**
7	**Earned Value Management Applied to Software**
8	**Metrics**
9	**Life Cycle Support**
10	**Lessons Learned**

3 Software Process Guidelines for Air Force Acquisition Organizations

3.1 Software Aspects of Acquisition Program Planning

Planning for software must address the system life cycle from inception through development, operations, and support, until system disposal. Whether the anticipated system development effort is a new program start involving a source selection or a delivery of additional incremental capability for a legacy program, proper planning ensures an executable program is defined and all required resources are available. Planning also provides a yardstick by which progress can be measured.

The acquisition program office must address all the software focus areas identified in AFI 63-1201. Three categories of software planning will be addressed here:

 a. Planning for Program Start (section 3.1.1)

 b. Planning for Acquisition/Development Program Execution (section 3.1.2)

 c. Planning for Post-Deployment Support (section 3.1.3)

In addition, critical elements of planning should be incorporated as appropriate in the program SEP or other program plans. Section 3.1.4 provides guidance for addressing CS&S related topics in the SEP.

See Appendix A, "Software in the Integrated Master Plan," for guidance on recommended software content in the IMP.

3.1.1 Planning for Program Start
Planning for Program Start/Source Selection should address the following activities:

 a. Developing a CS&S acquisition strategy consistent with the system acquisition strategy, including program objectives and constraints; available and projected assets, resources, and technologies such as non-developmental items (NDI); acquisition methods; potential contract types and terms; end user considerations; risk identification; life cycle support approach; technology insertion; and architecture & interoperability.

 b. Defining and establishing the membership and responsibilities for the Air Force organization that will be responsible for software (includes interaction with system developers, testers, supporters, and users; as well as the means of management and control of the CS&S development effort).

 c. Identifying and obtaining sufficient trained and experienced personnel to plan and oversee the computer system and software development.

 d. Identifying, capturing, documenting, and maturing end user/warfighter needs and requirements specific to CS&S.

 e. Identifying any policies, standards, or other guidance applicable to the program.

f. Identifying all software to be developed, reused (used-as-is), modified, integrated, tested, or delivered (includes operational software; tools for software development, integration, test, and data reduction; firmware; databases; software for mission planning, training, automated test, and other support equipment/functions).

g. Examine the range of potential architectural approaches and assess the risks and opportunities associated with each to arrive at initial system/software architecture.

h. Developing an early and independent program office estimate of the expected software size, effort (staff hours), cost, and schedule (prior to release of Request for Proposal (RFP) or receipt of offeror proposals).

i. Ensuring the planned CS&S development is consistent with the program budget and schedule allocated to software.

j. Developing CS&S inputs to the RFP.

Note that one method for organizing the program office and other Government stakeholders for the CS&S role in acquisition was defined by what used to be called the Computer Resources Working Group (CRWG). The CRWG typically functioned as an advisory body to the program manager. These functions would now be handled by a software IPT or perhaps a working group under the IPT. Typical responsibilities should include:

a. Advising the program or system manager in all areas relating to the acquisition and support of CS&S.

b. Developing and maintaining a Computer Resources Life Cycle Management Plan (CRLCMP).

c. Planning and implementing a CS&S post deployment support capability.

d. Monitoring CS&S development progress, and monitoring program compliance with any applicable CS&S policy, plans, procedures, and standards.

e. Integrating software test activities with the overall test program.

3.1.2 *Planning for Acquisition/Development Program Execution*

Planning for the System Development and Demonstration (SD&D) phase should include the following activities:

a. Identifying and obtaining sufficient trained and experienced personnel to oversee the CS&S development.

b. Ensuring the offeror/developer team possesses adequate capability and capacity (including processes, tools, and people).

c. Developing/evaluating the proposed application of evolutionary strategies for software development and capability delivery to match approved time-phased delivery of capability with resources and available technology (definition of block/increment capability content and related EMA).

d. Addressing the program approach to system and software requirements definition and management, including the use of collaborative communications and other methods to control software size growth due to derived requirements and design evolution.

e. Refining the identification of all software to be developed, reused (used-as-is), modified, integrated, tested, or delivered (includes operational software; commercial off-the-shelf

(COTS) and other NDI software, tools for software development, integration, test, and data reduction; firmware; databases; software for mission planning, training, automated test, and other support equipment/functions).

f. Accommodating the acquisition and software development issues related to the use of NDI, including COTS software, reuse software, and Government furnished software (GOTS).

g. Formulating and managing CS&S-related budgets and schedules, including initial estimates, revised estimates, and actuals for software size, effort (cost), and schedule.

h. Ensuring the planned CS&S development is consistent with the program budget and schedule allocated to software and the disciplined application of the proposed software development processes.

i. Identifying and managing the CS&S-related program risks.

j. Managing the CS&S development with appropriate insight and control through:

    (1) Integration of software engineering with the program's systems engineering process, including technical reviews, and engineering data and documentation.

    (2) Software metrics.

    (3) Government and contract requirements for Software Resources Data Reports (SRDRs) in accordance with DoD 5000.04-M-1, Cost and Software Data Reporting.

    (4) Application of EVM to software (measuring progress relative to planned discrete, measurable software events and work products with defined exit criteria).

    (5) Software content in the Integrated Master Plan (IMP), Integrated Master Schedule (IMS), System Engineering Plan (SEP), Test and Evaluation Master Plan (TEMP), and Work Breakdown Structure (WBS), to the lowest level of work managed.

    (6) Establishing, obtaining commitment to, and executing the program through the disciplined application of effective systems and software development processes, including establishing and monitoring commitment to developer software processes as documented in the Software Development Plan (SDP).

    (7) Maintaining appropriate insight into developer and subcontractor/supplier activities to ensure the processes being employed are effective in achieving the desired result.

k. Addressing contracting considerations for software, including:

    (1) Use of COTS software, open source software (OSS), Government furnished software (GFS), and other previously developed software.

    (2) Contract types for software development.

    (3) Software related contract clauses.

    (4) Software related contract deliverables.

    (5) Software related performance incentives appropriate to the program's challenges and life cycle phase (through Award Fee and Incentive Fee structures).

    (6) Intellectual property (IP) rights (including licenses).

(7) Coordination with Defense Contract Management Agency (DCMA).

l.   Ensuring an adequate approach for software security assurance, including:

(1) Identification of critical software technologies and protection techniques including strategies to comply with the Anti-Tamper (AT) and Software Protection Initiatives (SPI).

(2) Development of an information assurance strategy and requirements for Certification & Accreditation (C&A).

m. Planning and developing the post-deployment support capability for the CS&S, including software product engineering data (documentation) and intellectual property rights.

3.1.3 Planning for Post Deployment Support

The details of planning for post deployment support are addressed later in section 3.12.1. However, it is worth noting here that a CRLCMP is a good method for organizing and documenting such planning. The CRLCMP is no longer required by policy, but such a plan can still be developed to establish and document the buy-in of all stakeholders, including the end customer (e.g., Air Combat Command, Air Mobility Command), operational testers, and system sustainers. Items appropriate to be addressed in this plan include:

a.   Identification of responsibilities of the acquisition, developer, support, test, and user organizations in planning and implementing the software sustainment capability.

b.   Planned source of life cycle (post-deployment) software support and identification of the life cycle support infrastructure.

c.   Identification of computer systems hardware, software, documentation, and software engineering environment (as applicable) that will be delivered.

d.   Human resources required for software support with supporting assumptions and rationale.

e.   Intellectual property rights (including licenses).

f.   Software test and integration considerations, including responsibilities for various levels of test and integration of software, location and fidelity of test and integration laboratories, and required test assets.

g.   Transition of applicable operational software and support tools from the developer to the post deployment support organization.

h.   Interim support (if applicable) subsequent to the completion of system development but prior to the availability of the permanent post-deployment support capability.

i.   Security classification, certification, and accreditation considerations.

j.   Required facilities including buildings, integration labs, and test ranges.

3.1.4 Software Planning in the Systems Engineering Plan

The program SEP provides an opportunity to integrate CS&S planning with the overall systems engineering planning. The following paragraphs provide a mapping of software-related concerns to the SEP guidance, based on the OSD SEP Preparation Guide. Note: all comments below are references to Appendix B of the OSD SEP Guide, which contains the Sample Format for Milestone B, System Development and Demonstration.

----

a. Section 1.1, 2nd paragraph: For software, this includes:

    (1) Identification of computing system and software-related standards.

    (2) Addressing sustainment planning (capability and capacity needs) in order to balance overall software acquisition and sustainment costs.

    (3) Describing the program plan for determining the location of software sustainment activities, required personnel, software development and integration environments.

b. Section 2.3, last bullet: For computing systems and software, address such things as redundancy management and fault tolerance. Also address processor and computing system reserve capacity for throughput, memory, I/O.

c. Section 2.5, last bullet: Although not a perfect fit, for software this could include understanding the program approach to lessons learned, including how historical software size, growth, reuse, productivity rates, and developer capability have been used to ensure the current program is realistic and executable. All software (support software as well as prime mission equipment) must be addressed. The problem that repeatedly gets programs in trouble is expecting more performance than can be fit into the available program budget and schedule, or in other words, failing to ensure the program is realistic and executable. Address here the systems engineering role in defining a high confidence, low-to-moderate risk program that will allow us to deliver the required capability within the cost and schedule constraints.

d. Section 3.3, 1st bullet: For software, this means addressing:

    (1) How the program office will organize and staff to manage the software acquisition, including the required staffing, training, and experience levels.

    (2) The program plan to establish required support for specialized technology areas, such as information assurance or safety-critical systems.

e. Section 3.4, 2nd bullet: For software, this means describing the processes the program office will employ, as well as how the program office will support the disciplined application of established development processes by the contractor/developer team.

f. Section 3.4, 4th bullet: Not just for "systems integration," but for software, this means describing:

    (1) The program approach to identifying the mix of software to be developed, modified, reused, or purchased.

    (2) How it will be assured that proposed reuse components are mature and suitable for the intended use; there is a full disclosure/understanding of any projected modification needed; baseline and configuration management is in place; and associated regression testing, ownership rights and licensing, product assurance, and other risks have been addressed.

g. Section 3.5, 6th bullet: For software, this means understanding:

    (1) The approach the contractor/developer team and program office will use to establish and manage software development processes and to commit to their consistent use through the IMP, IMS, Statement of Work (SOW), and other documents such as the SDP.

(2) How the program office will ensure development processes are consistently employed.

(3) How supplier capability will be evaluated during source selection to determine strengths, weaknesses, and risks related to computing systems and software.

(4) How supplier capability will be evaluated when establishing software development/integration baselines and contracts.

h. Section 4.1: For software, this means describing the program approach, including computing system and software impacts, for incremental capability development, verification, and delivery/fielding.

i. Section 5: For software, this means identifying the critical software-related technical review content and associated entry and exit criteria, or identifying where this information can be located in other program documentation.

j. Section 6.1, 3rd bullet: Although not a perfect fit, for software this could include explaining the program approach to applying EVM at the software level to provide an objective measure of software cost and schedule performance.

k. Section 6.1, 4th bullet: For software, this means formally managing expectations for software-enabled capabilities by describing how the program will establish, with high confidence, that the cost, schedule, and technical (performance) baselines are compatible and achievable.

l. Section 6.1, 5th bullet: For software, this includes the overall program plan for software metrics, including:

(1) How metrics are established, collected, and employed to manage the program.

(2) How the Air Force core software metrics (size, effort, schedule, quality, requirements definition and stability, staffing, progress, and computer resources utilization) are used.

(3) How the program office will use metrics and other methods to maintain appropriate insight into the contractor/developer team software development status.

m. Section 6.3, 1st paragraph: For software, this means addressing software-related risks as part of the overall program approach to risk management. Specific attention should be given to addressing software estimating risks (underestimating size or growth, reuse erosion, less than expected productivity (more hours than expected per line of code), and undefined requirements.) as well as other computing system and software risks.

3.1.5   Sources of Additional Guidance

a. <u>SEI Software Acquisition Planning Guidelines</u>: Provides guidance on software acquisition planning and strategy on 13 different topics, including open systems approach, COTS-based systems, software architecture, software sustainment, requirements development, requirements management, operational information assurance, information assurance for COTS sustainment, information asset protection, software testing, software risk management, software metrics, and software-based award fees.

3.2 *Estimating Software Size, Effort and Schedule*

Software estimation is an inexact science. The data input to the process is usually highly uncertain, and where commercial estimating models are concerned, Dr. Barry Boehm in his book *Software Engineering Economics* states that "a software cost estimation model is doing well if it can estimate software development costs within 20% of the actual costs, 70% of the time, and on its home turf (that is, within the class of projects to which it is calibrated)."

The challenge then is to comply with Air Force policy that requires estimating and funding acquisition programs with high (80-90%) confidence. That is to say, programs are to be estimated and funded so that the total program costs for any given program would be within the budget 80-90% of the time. Also, program milestones and program completion should meet the planned schedule 80-90% of the time. Air Force programs that involve intensive software development have a poor record of satisfying cost, schedule, and performance expectations.

Independent Government software estimates must be developed to facilitate realistic program planning, set reasonable expectations, support evaluations of offeror proposed costs and schedules during source selection or the start of new development blocks for legacy programs, and facilitate monitoring contract execution. These estimates must be developed to the highest confidence achievable given the state of the known requirements and any other data that characterizes the program at the time the estimate is performed.

In addition to estimates at program start, an Estimate to Complete (ETC) or Estimate at Completion (EAC) is periodically needed in order to support an independent program evaluation or to otherwise determine program financial condition. Much of the guidance provided herein can also be applied to determining the content remaining in a program in order to formulate an ETC or EAC or support of an Integrated Baseline Review (IBR). How often a program performs such estimates is dependent upon program needs.

The high degree of uncertainty at program start-up and in early development program phases makes software estimation with high confidence extremely difficult. The following factors contribute to this difficulty:

   a. Software size estimates and supporting information are often provided by developers/offerors in a competitive environment, which promotes overly optimistic estimates.

   b. Acquisition organizations may be inclined to accept optimistic estimates when even those optimistic estimates strain the planned program budget and schedule.

   c. Development organizations assume the best people, or new/improved processes or tools, will lead to unrealistic productivity improvements.

   d. New systems usually involve development of unprecedented systems/capabilities.

   e. System performance is typically stated in high-level terms that are not directly translatable to software requirements and associated software size.

   f. It is common to make erroneous and optimistic assumptions about initial software size, software size growth during development, software reuse, and non developmental software (NDS) for large, complex, and unprecedented systems.

   g. There is an unrealistic expectation of accuracy in the results from the chosen estimating models and methods.

   h. The program being estimated may not fit the chosen estimating models and methods.

i. Programs that are divided into many increments may not allocate sufficient effort for integrating new development with the baseline.

j. Requirements that are not well understood may not be allocated to the software until later in the program.

k. Long development phases for large, complex programs provide ample opportunity for outside forces to impact the program (funding instability, requirements changes).

This section provides additional guidance on developing high confidence estimates, dealing with software estimation risks, software estimation process considerations, and establishing realistic program baselines for software. The objective is to develop estimates that are based on the best available information, while fully disclosing and accounting for uncertainties. Throughout the estimation process, the Government must demonstrate unwavering commitment, and must make clear to all potential offerors its intent to develop and apply realistic estimates in establishing executable program baselines.

3.2.1 High Confidence Program Criteria

The 2006 Defense Acquisition Performance Assessment (DAPA) report notes that "...current acquisition strategies encourage a 'Conspiracy of Hope' that introduces instability at the very beginning of acquisition programs. The 'Conspiracy of Hope' occurs when industry is encouraged to propose unrealistic cost, optimistic performance and understate technical risk estimates during the acquisition solicitation process and the Department is encouraged to accept these proposals as the foundation for program baselines."

The DAPA report defines "high confidence" as a program with an 80 percent chance of completing development at or below estimated cost. AFI 63-1201 specifically states in Attachment 8, paragraph 8.1.1: "Estimate software development and integration at high (80-90%) confidence levels."

At the program level, high confidence can be addressed in a number of areas. A very top-level summary of results from an Aeronautical Systems Center (ASC) Balanced Scorecard Integrated Product Team (IPT) on High Confidence Program Criteria is provided here:

a. Requirements: There is a preliminary/draft Capabilities Definition Document (CDD) available for at least a year prior to Milestone B with no significant content issues, all requirements have been identified and are incorporated into a traceability tool, requirements trade-space is well defined, and the technical approach is well-defined and mature.

b. Expectation Management Agreement (EMA): An EMA that has honestly assessed all requirements, other than Key Performance Parameters (KPPs), for realism within the available budget and schedule and is consistent with the Program Management Document (PMD) in place, there is an established cutoff date for requirements changes, the using command has committed to funding the program at the 90% confidence level, and there is a realistic block/incremental approach.

c. Cost/Funding: The currently approved funding matches the 90% confidence estimate or there is a viable plan to obtain additional funding to match.

d. Program Risk Management/Health: An Integrated Risk Assessment (IRA) has been completed prior to the Software Design Document (SDD) Acquisition Strategy Panel (ASP).

e. <u>Acquisition Strategy</u>: A Milestone A or Pre-Milestone B phase has occurred prior to the ASP for the SD&D contract.

f. <u>Integrated Master Schedule (IMS)</u>: A realistic/high level IMS has been used to formulate acquisition strategy, IMS durations are based on realistic timelines and logical entrance/exit criteria (not arbitrary dates), the IMS accounts for internal/external dependencies, and the schedule includes quantification of risks.

g. <u>Systems Engineering (SE)</u>: Robust SE planning is ongoing, a sound SE management approach is being taken, and the technical baseline is established and under control.

h. <u>Contract/Incentives</u>: Contract performance incentives are being utilized, the contract type has been appropriately selected to fairly apportion risk between the Government and contractor, and contract options are events-based.

i. <u>Resources</u>: The Government program office staffing plan is in place and on schedule.

j. <u>Socialization</u>: A plan is in place to socialize the program with HQ AFMC, SAF/AQ, HQ AF, and OSD staffs as appropriate.

For more information on the IPT results see the presentation "Focus Week Training: High Confidence Programs."

Note that while these criteria are defined at the program level, there are software level concerns related to several of these areas. For example, program level performance requirements may be considered stable and complete, however typically several levels of design and requirements evolution stand between the top level system requirements and the software level requirements and design as shown in FIGURE 1. The systems engineering process evolves these system level requirements into the detailed subsystem designs (perhaps through multiple levels of subsytems) and ultimately into the software requirements and design. It is only at this point of understanding the software requirements that the real size of the software development effort can be determined. This drives associated impacts on schedule, resources, and cost/funding.

The difficulty in achieving accurate software estimates early in a development effort is illustrated in FIGURE 2. In his pioneering book on software estimating, "Software Engineering Economics," Barry W. Boehm addresses the topic of software cost estimation accuracy. He concludes that the level of knowledge about the software being estimated is highly dependent on the life-cycle phase of the software development. Subjectively, in the early stages of determining feasibility, the uncertainty can be as much as a factor of four on either the high or low side. By the time a software requirements specification is developed, the uncertainty drops to a factor of about 1.5 in either direction. By the time product design is completed, the software estimate uncertainty should be down to about 1.25, at which point the author states that a good program manager can generally turn a software effort estimate into a self-fulfilling prophecy.

This thinking is consistent with that of Ms. Sue Payton, U.S. Air Force Acquisition Executive, who has stated: "One of the best ways to improve USAF cost estimates is to wait until a preliminary design review has been completed, rather than trying to guess a weapon's price before the final requirements are defined."

Additional factors that contribute to high confidence from a software point of view include:

a. The estimate is based upon well-defined, stable requirements.

b. The estimate is based upon a comprehensive, detailed, well-documented software development schedule with durations and logic.

c. Actual software size (in lines of code or function points), as well as productivity and cost data, is available from the same program or a very analogous program at the same developer facility, using the same or similar processes and tools, and personnel of equivalent capability.

d. The estimate includes appropriate factors for historical experience for software size growth, reuse, and these factors can be validated.

e. Statistical techniques have been used to determine the 80-90% values of the cost and schedule cumulative probability functions.

f. The estimate has been independently reviewed and cross-checked.

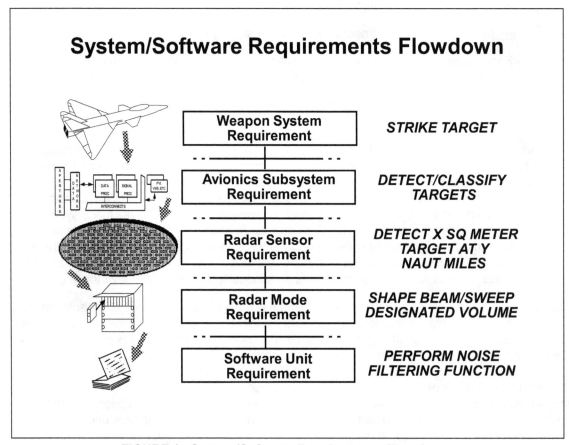

FIGURE 1. System/Software Requirements Flowdown.

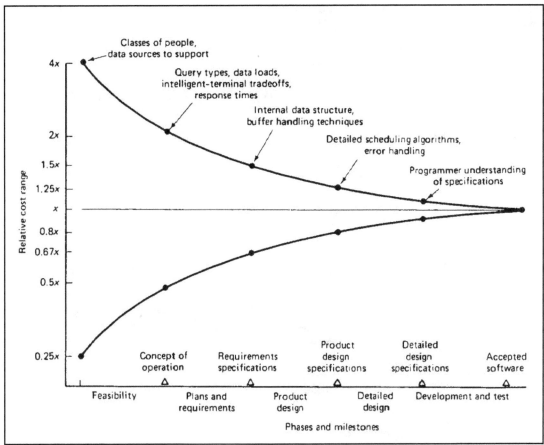

NOTE: Tailored from "Software Engineering Economics," Prentice Hall, Barry W. Boehm, 1981.

FIGURE 2. Software Cost Estimation Accuracy vs Phase.

3.2.2   Software Estimation Risks

One of the most significant risks faced by any weapon system program with a significant software component is the ability to properly estimate the software size, effort, and schedule. These and other inherent uncertainties related to software must be addressed as risks as part of the estimation process. The following factors contribute to software estimation risk:

a. Ability to properly estimate the size of the software development and integration effort, given the known state of software-level requirements at the time of the estimate.

b. Ability to prevent or account for growth due to developer derived requirements and design evolution.

c. Ability to achieve expected levels of software NDI, including COTS and reuse.

d. Ability to generate accurate estimates for modifying and integrating existing (reused) software.

e. Ability to effectively manage requirements and changes, which results in software size growth and adversely impacts effort and schedule estimates.

f. Developer capability, including people, processes, plans, and historical productivity.

g. Ability to develop software at the expected productivity rate.

Another view of the factors that affect the ability to estimate software with high confidence is provided in FIGURE 3.

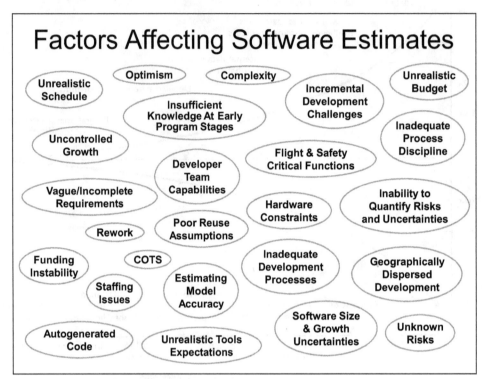

FIGURE 3. Factors Affecting Software Estimate.

At the time initial estimates are accomplished for most embedded systems, there is only a very high-level understanding of the detailed design and specific software implementation that will be required to implement the desired system performance. Commercial estimating models such as Parametric Review of Information for Costing and Evaluation – Software (PRICE-S) and System Evaluation and Estimation of Resource – Software Estimation Models (SEER-SEM) are primarily driven by the size of the software, however there is considerable uncertainty in the process of determining the size of software to deliver a capability that has not been developed before. Consequently, the size estimate is normally developed by considering the size of similar past projects as well as expert opinion. If this initial size estimate is too small (the normal situation), then it is likely that the resulting software effort (cost) and schedule baselines will also be too small, and this will eventually cause significant program impact.

The challenge in building realistic cost and schedule estimates early in a program is largely due to the fact that up-front estimates are based on numerous assumptions and uncertainties.

Several iterations of cost and schedule estimation may be necessary to converge on a more accurate estimate as the software product matures. The engineering role is to provide the most accurate technical information (both assumptions and facts) available in order to create a realistic program software development baseline.

The size of the software typically grows during development. Part of this growth can be attributed to inadequate initial size estimates, but growth also comes about because of the improved understanding of the size of the software effort that is gained as the design of the system and software evolves. There is evidence to suggest that routine growth in software size over the course of the SD&D phase can be 100%. Various numbers have been suggested over the years, but accounting for growth in the estimates for software components should be dependent on a component-by-component review of the type of software involved. FIGURE 4 shows the history of software growth at one Air Force product center.

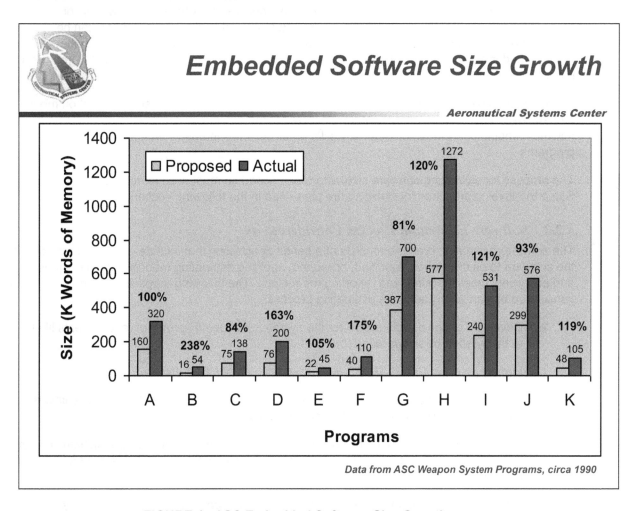

FIGURE 4. ASC Embedded Software Size Growth.

There is also evidence to suggest that about two-thirds to three-fourths of the software growth typically encountered is a result of this improved understanding of the size of the job.

Software reuse is the source of another significant estimation risk. Historically, Air Force programs typically fall well short of realizing the benefit from software reuse expected at the outset. This results in a need for additional software effort in order to provide the required functionality.

Another software estimation risk factor involves the commercial parametric models commonly used for developing software estimates, whose knowledge bases have been built up over time based on more classical software development of unique software code. Today's systems often involve much more integration of existing code (commercial and reused components) rather than development of new code. Since these types of systems are more current and not yet as numerous as the classic uniquely developed software systems that drive the models, it is quite possible that these current systems are not as closely fit to the existing models. It certainly requires more modeling expertise to properly model and estimate these systems.

Developer capability is yet another estimation risk factor, and is closely related to the developer's ability to produce software at the predicted rate. It is tempting and easy for offerors in a source selection environment to claim expected productivity improvements based on new tools or processes, or a more highly skilled and experienced staff, and to some extent these can be factors in program performance. But the productivity experienced on real programs is what matters, and this productivity will not likely differ significantly (i.e., more than 5% - 10%) from past productivity levels at the same developer location.

Several if not all of the software-related risks listed at the beginning of this section exist on most embedded system acquisition programs. Risks related to original size, growth, and reuse as a minimum should be included as standard risks on all software-intensive weapon system programs.

The process for estimating software size, effort, and schedule must account for these risks. Some top-level approaches for doing so are presented in the following section.

3.2.3   Software Estimation Process Considerations

The software estimating process consists of a series of activities that include estimating size of the software to be developed, modified, or reused; applying estimating models and techniques; and analyzing, crosschecking, and reporting the results. The following steps should be considered as part of any software estimating process:

a.   Develop a notional architecture for the system, and identify program requirements likely to be satisfied by software.

b.   Identify potential COTS, GOTS, and other sources of NDI software.

c.   Identify existing software that will be modified, including the size of the overall software as well as the size of the expected modifications.

d.   Identify software that will be newly developed for this program to provide functionality not available from existing software, or to adapt/integrate all the necessary software components.

e.   Obtain software size information for all software elements, where size is carefully defined and measured in one of the two standard software size measures: non-comment source lines of code (SLOC) or function points.

f.   Assess the uncertainty in the new and modified software sizes, based on historical data (if available) and engineering judgment.

g.   Assess the uncertainty associated with the reusability of existing software (COTS, GOTS, and NDI) in the context of the program (see section 3.2.4). Estimate the trade studies, familiarization, and the integration and testing efforts required to accommodate the unmodified reused code.

h.   Account for software complexity and the proposed development approach/processes, and assess any overlaps in software builds.

i.   Be realistic about expected software productivity and any assumption of significantly higher than historical productivity due to applying the best people, improved/more efficient processes, or new and improved development tools. Past performance, where actual size, cost, and productivity data is available at the same developer facility for the same program or a very analogous program, should be heavily weighted. It is rare to have the A-team people for a long-duration embedded system development, and new processes and tools often fall short of expectations.

j. Apply growth factors to new/modified and reuse software, based on past experience and the level of uncertainty.

k. Account for all remaining uncertainties as estimate risks (see section 3.2.2).

l. Ensure the estimate includes software support to systems engineering, system and sub-system requirements definition, configuration management, quality assurance, program management, system integration, and system test as appropriate.

m. Address the software development life-cycle from software requirements analysis through software-related system integration and testing. The chosen modeling/estimation approach may not address the entire software effort since some commercial parametric models focus on the period starting with the baseline set of software requirements and ending with a fully integrated and tested subsystem / functional software product ready for software / hardware integration and test. Estimate and include any additional effort required to develop, allocate, and analyze the subsystem and software requirements; perform software to hardware (subsystem) integration and test; and perform system integration and test.

n. Crosscheck estimate results with other methods such as other models, expert advice, rules of thumb, and historical productivity.

o. Improve the estimate over time.

3.2.4 *Estimating Reuse Feasibility*

New systems often involve significant reuse of various software artifacts (i.e., requirements, design, code, and test data). The percentage of software being proposed for reuse has grown from 20%, to 60%, to 80% or more. Some current embedded systems involve nearly 100% reuse of existing systems and software components. This is not in line with Air Force experience, and the classic estimating approaches that rely on an estimate of the size of the software to be newly developed or modified, adjusted for growth, may not be applicable.

In addition, experience shows that actual reuse achieved often falls far short of the reuse expected at the outset of an embedded system development program. Part of this is likely due to the late understanding about what is really required from the reuse software, and part is likely due to the growth in software that must be developed to achieve the full expected functionality, or to interface/integrate the reuse software into the rest of the system.

While the full understanding of reuse components occurs well into the system/software design process, there are a number of attributes that can be examined at the start of a development. FIGURE 5 identifies reuse assessment attributes as portrayed by Dr. Barry Boehm in his book *Software Cost Estimating With COCOMO II*.

Another problem with dealing with proposed reuse in early estimates is that for new or modified code, offeror software size is normally inflated at some percentage in accordance with technical risk assessments, to account for the software growth that normally occurs during embedded systems software development. Since there can be little, or in some cases almost zero, code being developed or modified when very high levels of reuse are proposed, this inflation/growth technique breaks down.

COTS/Reuse Assessment Attributes

Correctness
accuracy
correctness

Availability/Robustness
availability
fail safe
fail soft
fault tolerance
input error tolerance
redundancy
reliability
robustness
safety

Security
access related
sabotage related

Product Performance
execution performance
Information / data capacity
precision
memory performance
response time
throughput

Understandability
documentation quality
simplicity
testability

Ease of Use
usability / human factors

Version Compatibility
downward compatibility
upward compatibility

Intercomponent Compatibility
with other components
interoperability

Flexibility
extendability
flexibility

Installation / Upgrade Ease
installation ease
upgrade / refresh ease

Portability
portability

Functionality
functionality

Price
initial purchase or lease
recurring costs

Maturity
product maturity
vendor maturity

Vendor Support
response time for critical problem
support
warranty

Training
user training

Vendor Concessions
will escrow code
will make modifications

From *Software Cost Estimation With COCOMO II*, by Barry Boehm

FIGURE 5. COTS/Reuse Assessment Attributes.

An alternate approach for assessing risk and determining potential growth in the amount of software to be developed and modified where there is significant proposed reuse is shown in FIGURE 6. This approach considers a number of attributes to assess the risk that additional software will have to be developed. The size of the assumed new development is based on the size of the software to be reused, as well as evaluator confidence in developers' reuse claims. Once the assessment of these attributes has determined the associated risk and growth potential, the growth is applied and the estimate can be adjusted accordingly.

The Government Accountability Office (GAO) offers additional insight regarding the risks associated with reuse and COTS software. The July 2007 Exposure Draft of GAO's *Cost Assessment Guide – Best practices for Estimating and Managing Program Costs*, states the following:

"Reused and autogenerated software source lines of code should be differentiated from the total count. Both reused and autogenerated software provides the developer with code that can be used in a new program, but neither comes for free and additional effort is usually associated with incorporating them into a new program. For instance, the effort associated with reused code depends on whether significant integration, reverse engineering, and additional design, validation, and testing are required. But if the effort to incorporate reused software is too great, it may be cheaper to write the code from scratch. Assumptions regarding savings from reused and autogenerated code should be looked at skeptically because of the additional work to research the code and provide necessary quality checks."

Reuse Risk & Growth

Attribute	Low Risk (0-5% Growth)	Moderate Risk (6-15% Growth)	High Risk (16-25% Growth)
Maturity	The software is operational in a similar mission application and architecture	The software is in lab or flight test and is not yet operational, or requires architectural adaptation	The software is under development and has not been lab or flight tested
Performance	Performance and interface requirements are verified to be identical	There are some differences in performance and/or interface requirements	There are significant differences in performance and/or interface requirements
Integration Complexity	Integration is not complex and software can be used essentially "as-is" with little or no development	Integration involves minor, localized modifications with moderate complexity	Significant or complex modification or development is required, and/or changes are dispersed
Quality	The software is free of known defects	The software has minor / non-critical limitations or defects	The software has critical limitations or defects that must be corrected
Control	The offeror has full control over the future evolution of the software	The offeror has limited control over the future evolution of the software	The offeror has no control over the future evolution of the software
Access	The offeror has full access to the source code	The offeror has limited access to the source code	The offeror has no access to the source code
Familiarity	The offeror has significant familiarity or experience with the software	The offeror has some familiarity or experience with the software	The offeror has little or no familiarity or experience with the software
Property Rights & Licenses	Adequate property rights & licenses are established	There are uncertainties with property rights / licenses	There are known issues with property rights / licenses
Approach	Proposed approach for achieving predicted reuse is sound, and planned verification is adequate	Proposed approach for achieving predicted reuse is generally sound, with some open issues	Proposed approach for achieving predicted reuse is not substantiated, or planned verification is inadequate
Process	The offeror has an institutionalized process for making reuse decisions	The offeror has an informal process for making reuse decisions	The offeror has no documented process for making reuse decisions

FIGURE 6. Reuse Attributes Risk Growth.

In addition, the same GAO guide states the following regarding COTS software:

"It is wrong to think that commercial software will necessarily be a cheap solution. Estimators tend to underestimate the effort that comes before and after implementing off-the-shelf software. For example, requirements definition, design, and testing of the overall system must still be conducted. Poorly defined requirements can result in less than optimal software selection, necessitating the development of new code to satisfy all requirements. This unexpected effort will raise costs and cause program delays. In addition, adequate training and access to detailed documentation are important for effectively using the software. Furthermore, since commercial software is subject to intense market forces, upgrades can be released with minimal testing, causing unpredictable problems, such as defects and system incompatibilities. When this happens, additional time is needed to analyze the cause of failures and fix them. Finally, interfaces between the software and other applications may need to be rewritten every time the software is upgraded. While software developers can address all these issues, they take some time to accomplish. Therefore, adequate planning should be identified and estimated by the cost estimator to ensure that enough time and resources are available to perform them."

3.2.5 *Realistic Program Baselines for Software*

Nothing has done more to undermine acquisition credibility and complicate effective management of the acquisition of software intensive systems than the inability to establish realistic software development cost and schedule baselines. Without a realistic estimate of the required effort and schedule, tied to specific requirements during program formulation and adjusted for risk, it is almost a certainty that the initial overall program estimate will not accommodate the software development. Likewise, if an estimate is not available when proposals are evaluated in source selection, there is no basis from which to judge the feasibility of the offerors' proposed effort and schedule. Programs established with unexecutable cost and schedule baselines will inevitably be forced to cut corners along the way or will fail to deliver the promised performance with available funds and within the program schedule.

As discussed earlier in this section, the challenge in building realistic cost and schedule baselines early comes from the fact that up-front estimates during program planning and formulation are based on numerous assumptions and uncertainties. Several iterations of the cost and schedule estimates, as the program progresses toward Source Selection, may be necessary to converge on a more accurate estimate. The solicitation and incorporation of data characterizing each offeror's proposed system into the estimate further supports achieving a high confidence estimate and resultant realistic program baseline. The engineering role is to provide the most accurate technical information (both assumptions and facts) available in order to create a realistic program software development baseline.

To review, the steps to arrive at a realistic cost and schedule baseline include the following:

a. Develop initial software cost and schedule estimates to the highest confidence achievable given what is known about the program at the time the estimate is performed. Use these estimates during initial program planning and formulation.

b. Refine those initial estimates as more data becomes available during the pre-RFP time period.

c. Solicit data and design details during Source Selection and use those refined estimates to evaluate the realism of the offeror's proposed cost and schedule baselines.

d. Develop and refine estimates of software size for all software to be developed and integrated. Include expected reuse and integration of legacy software, subcontractor efforts, COTS, and Government furnished equipment (GFE). Base these estimates on similar past programs when possible.

e. Use estimated size to establish the associated software development effort and schedule (this may include defining appropriate software estimating model input parameters). Collaborate with other Government organizations to create and maintain program estimates.

f. During Source Selection, ensure the proposed effort and schedule are compatible with disciplined application of the offeror's proposed software development processes, accommodates the required system performance (relates to software size), and accommodates requirements changes, including the reallocation of requirements from hardware to software.

g. Ensure the key deliverables and activities are clearly addressed in the contract.

h. Identify and manage software-related risks.

i. Ensure that cost, schedule, and technical/performance baselines are realistic and compatible with established program requirements.

j.   Ensure that expectations related to software are managed in accordance with the overall program's EMA.

k.   Ensure the program cost and schedule baselines have the capacity to accommodate the high confidence estimates for effort and schedule, as well as potential risk impacts.

3.2.6   Sources of Additional Guidance

a.   "*Software Estimating Rules of Thumb*," Capers Jones, 20 March 2007.

b.   The Poor Person's Guide to Estimating Software Development Costs, IEEE ReadyNotes, Donald J. Reifer, 2006.

c.   "*Software Estimation Perspectives*", Barry W. Boehm & Richard E Fairley, IEEE Software, Nov-Dec 2000.

d.   "*Liar, Fool, or Both?*," Robert Charette.

e.   "*How Software Estimating Tools Work*," Capers Jones, 27 February 2005.

f.   Cost Assessment Guide (Exposure Draft), GAO, July 2007.

> *"One clear message from software cost and schedule models is that larger amounts of developed software require larger amounts of budget and schedules. ... It's better to tell your customers that they can expect either a "fixed amount of software" or a "fixed cost or schedule," but not both."*
>
> *Barry Boehm*
> *"The Art of Expectations Management"*
> *IEEE Computer, January 2000*

> *"Historically, we have designed our programs with a 60-70% confidence level. If we are to build credibility with both the user and Congress we must change this paradigm by establishing a goal of having at least a 90% confidence level in meeting our commitments."*
>
> *Dr. Marvin R. Sambur, formerly SAF/AQ*
> *Policy Memo 03A-006*
> *29 April 2003*

> *"We want to make really sure when we decide how much a program will cost...that we're confident it is accurate. If we really knew the cost was going to go up, would we even start the program? We've got to get it right, or acquisition gets a black eye."*
>
> *Sue Payton, SAF/AQ*

3.3 Management of Software Related Risks

Risk is a potential (uncertain) future event that has negative consequences. In acquisition, the risk event or consequence is often related to not achieving program objectives. Risk management is the art or practice of controlling risk, by identifying and tracking risk areas, performing periodic risk assessments to determine risks and their potential impact, developing risk mitigation plans, and continuously monitoring and managing risks. The key to risk management success is early planning, aggressive execution, and an integrated approach that involves performance, cost, and schedule.

Risk management is performed over the life of the program and should involve the entire program team, including the contractor. Risk management in the development phase should start by revisiting any pre-award risk identification activities to assess the continued validity of the risks and to alter as necessary any mitigation strategies based on program progress. Note that in terms of handling identified risks, a program manager may decide to do nothing (accept the risk), or mitigate the risk (take action to prevent, reduce the probability and/or severity, or eliminate the risk). If a risk cannot be reasonably mitigated, then a response action should be planned to identify what will be done if the risk occurs. It should also be noted that mitigation plans often involve expenditure of resources, so in this event there should be a reasonable return on investment.

A program with effective risk management will exhibit the following characteristics:

    a. Appropriately tailored risk management strategies are defined and implemented.

    b. Potential problems (risks) that could impact project success are identified.

    c. The likelihood and consequences of these risks are understood.

    d. A priority order in which risks should be addressed is established.

    e. Mitigation alternatives appropriate for each potential problem are carefully considered based on project circumstances.

Software risk management should be integrated with the overall program approach to risk management. Software risks should be tracked as part of the overall risk activity, and should be a continuous focus of the integrated acquisition and developer software team(s). The rest of this section identifies a number of potential software related risks.

3.3.1 Standard Software Risks

Some software-related risks are so prevalent that they should be addressed on every program with significant software content. These are risks that can be addressed to some extent by the proper attention up front, but while such attention may reduce the level of risk, the only thing that can fully eliminate these risks is the maturing of the understanding of the system and related design over time. Risks that fall into this category include:

    a. Ability to properly estimate the software size and account for growth during development.

    b. Software reuse (if not achieved as planned, can also increase the size of the software development).

    c. Performance (the degree of uncertainty that the software will meet its requirements).

    d. Support (the degree of uncertainty that the resultant software will be maintainable).

Software size and reuse erosion risks typically linger at least until the subsystem designs and related software requirements are complete, and can even be adversely affected by the completion of the software design. An increase in the overall software development/integration size or erosion of the planned software reuse (which most likely also results in increase in the size) are early indicators that the planned software effort and schedule baselines are in jeopardy.

3.3.2 Other Typical Software Related Risks

The large number of potential software risks contributes to the difficulty of adequately managing these risks. While this is not an exhaustive list, the following risks have adversely affected multiple weapon system acquisition programs. Different mitigation strategies for these risks may be appropriate depending on the characteristics of specific programs:

a. Incompatible software development performance, effort, and schedule baselines.

b. Planned rapid staff buildup at the start of new development programs.

c. Complex, poorly defined, incomplete, or unstable system or software requirements.

d. Hand-off of software requirements from systems engineering without adequate interaction.

e. Inability to agree on and control block/increment content (also known as lack of a baseline).

f. COTS/GOTS availability, suitability, integration, and sustainment (consider the problem of coordination and integration of new releases every eight or nine months, as well as loss of support for COTS software products after roughly three new releases, over the relatively long development cycles of most weapon system programs).

g. Integration-heavy effort (significant integration effort for existing components).

h. Concurrent hardware development or requirements that drive the use of unproven tools or technology.

i. Extensive security requirements (as in multi-level security), which drive the use of immature technology.

j. Unprecedented system and software architectures.

k. Long-duration development timeframes (which provide more opportunity for external factors to affect the program).

l. Technical obsolescence of computing architectures and hardware.

m. Safety-critical requirements.

n. Uncontrolled, unknown, or untrusted sources of software (foreign developers, open source).

o. GFE or GFS with unknown performance capability.

p. Use of tools, methods, and technologies with which the developer has no previous experience.

q. A developer or developer team that is attempting to build systems outside their normal domains/experience.

r.   Multiple developers and subcontractors teaming to develop complex software intensive systems which must be tailored and integrated into a total system capability.

Two primary resources are available to help weapon system programs manage acquisition risks. The *"Risk Management Guide For DoD Acquisition"* provides Department of Defense (DoD)-level guidance, and *"AFMC Pamphlet 63-101, Risk Management"* provides command-level guidance.

3.3.3   Sources of additional guidance:

a.   DoD Acquisition Technology & Logistics (AT&L) Acquisition Community Connection *Risk Management Community of Practice*.

b.   ISO/IEC 16085 (IEEE Standard 16085-2006): *"Systems and Software Engineering – Life Cycle Processes – Risk Management."*

c.   *"The Program Manager's Guide to Software Acquisition Best Practices"*: Guidance published by the Software Program Manager's Network.

d.   *"Formal Risk Management:"* A Data Analysis Center for Software (DACS) Gold Practice.

e.   "*Assessment and Control of Software Risks*", Prentice Hall, Capers Jones, 1994: The author presents a detailed discussion of numerous software risk factors.

f.   "*Positive and Negative Innovations in Software Engineering*", Capers Jones, 2006.

3.4 Source Selection Considerations

This section addresses the CS&S tasks related to source selection, which include:

a. Creating the appropriate CS&S content for the RFP.

b. Accomplishing the evaluation of the submitted proposals, including assessing compliance with RFP requirements and determining the proposal risk associated with the offeror's approach.

This section also discusses the evaluation of offeror team capability, which is a significant part of the source selection process.

It is the Air Force's objective to select developers with sound approaches; applicable domain experience in the development of software-intensive systems; proven program management, systems engineering, and software engineering processes; and successful and relevant past performance. Therefore, the source selection strategy for CS&S is to solicit and evaluate proposal information with a focus in the following areas:

a. *Soundness of the proposed CS&S approach*, including CS&S architecture, and software development and integration approach.

b. *Offeror capability*, as defined by internal process standards that form the foundation for and can be tailored to provide program-specific processes, evidence that the proposed processes are part of the company culture, and capable, adequate staffing and other resources.

c. *Offeror commitment to the application of program-specific processes*, as defined in the Software Development Plan (SDP), IMP, IMS, and other contractual documents.

d. *Realistic program effort and schedule baselines* that are compatible with the estimated software development/integration effort and schedule, and that accommodate the consistent application of the proposed processes and tools.

e. *Successful past performance in software development*, including application of the proposed processes and satisfaction of program cost, schedule, and performance baselines. [Note: this topic is addressed in the Past Performance Evaluation.]

3.4.1 Software-Related Content in the Request for Proposal

Software is addressed in the RFP in order to solicit proposals that provide the information to support an effective Government evaluation and identification of strengths, deficiencies, uncertainties, weaknesses, and risks related to software. This section deals with the software content for the Statement of Objectives (SOO) and/or SOW as well as RFP Sections L (Instructions, Conditions and Notices to Offerors) and M (Evaluation Factors for Award).

The System Requirements Document (SRD), draft specification, or equivalent, should incorporate unique software requirements which are evidenced at the system level. This typically includes any user sourced requirements as well as typical computing system reserve capacity, growth, and architecture requirements. These requirements are then reflected as appropriate in the RFP.

The SOO is a top-level Government description of what is required by the solicitation, based on the content of the Initial Capability Document (ICD) or the Operational Requirements Document (ORD) as well as any applicable direction that has been given to the program team. The sole purpose of the SOO is to communicate to industry the Government's most important desired outcomes in the performance of the effort. The SOW may be generated by the offerors in response to the SOO. Or, the Government may develop a top-level SOW and in response the offerors provide a Contractor SOW (CSOW) as part of the proposal. The SOW/CSOW describes the tasks that must be performed and the conditions under which they must be performed. The SOW/CSOW should, at a minimum, include requirements to:

a. Define a software architecture and development approach appropriate for all computer software to be developed, integrated, and delivered under this solicitation.

b. Document the software development approach and related processes in a Software Development Plan (SDP), maintain the SDP, and comply with the SDP for all software developed under this solicitation throughout the development effort (refer to Appendix I for additional SDP content suggestions).

c. Support program office integrated product teams and working groups.

d. Provide software engineering management and control to ensure all software activities are conducted in accordance with the contractor's approved SDP and software engineering processes.

e. Conduct technical reviews to verify that the software products meet requirements and are suitable for intended use.

f. Collect, analyze, and report software metrics data, including at a minimum the Air Force core metrics (refer to Appendix H).

g. Maintain consistency among software products (e.g., requirements, architecture, design, code, test cases).

h. Plan the blocks/increments and the requirements to be met in each block/increment.

i. Plan, manage, and conduct the integration, regression, and qualification testing of software items for each block/increment.

j. Support system, segment, and subsystem requirements flowdown and allocate requirements to software items.

k. Maintain the integrity of the segment-wide software products and their configuration management.

RFP Section L describes the specific information that must be included in the proposals, while RFP Section M conveys the weighted selection standards to be utilized in the evaluation process and ultimately in the selection of the winning offeror or offeror team.

The Air Force Federal Acquisition Regulation Supplement (AFFARS) Section 5315 defines the "discriminators" reflected in the evaluation factors as the "significant aspects of an acquisition that are expected to distinguish one proposal from another, thus having an impact on the ultimate selection decision." Section M should contain distinct discriminators for software. Once Section M discriminators have been established, Section L is developed to ensure the information necessary to evaluate the factors and subfactors is requested in the proposal, and that information that will not be evaluated is not requested. The information in Section L must be developed in conjunction with Section M, and there must be complete correlation between Sections L and M in the final RFP.

Each proposal is evaluated against Section L requirements using Section M criteria to identify and document software-related strengths, deficiencies, uncertainties, weaknesses, and risks. The source selection evaluation is strictly limited to the evaluation factors and basis for award disclosed to the offerors in Section M of the RFP.

Section L should require submittal of a proposed SDP to document the software development processes proposed for use on the program. The SDP will be evaluated during source selection, and after contract award it should be updated as appropriate and submitted as a Contract Data Requirements List (CDRL) item for approval.

Refer to the following appendices for additional guidance on RFP content related to software:

a. Appendix B: Software-Related Content for the Statement of Objectives (SOO) / Statement of Work (SOW).

b. Appendix C: Example Software Content for Request for Proposal (RFP) Section L, Instructions, Conditions, and Notices to Offerors.

c. Appendix D: Example Software Content for Request for Proposal (RFP) Section M, Evaluation Factors for Award.

d. Appendix E: Contracting Considerations for Software.

The example content provided in Appendices C & D is extensive, especially for Section L (Appendix C). While the case cannot be made that each of these potential items/factors/subfactors are discriminators individually, collectively they form the basis for demonstrating that effective processes are established, and such processes have proven to be a critical element in the successful development of large, complex software systems.

Note again that RFP Sections L and M must be consistent. Example content in Appendices C and D is not organized in a consistent manner, and is provided simply for consideration in developing RFPs for specific programs.

3.4.2   Activities During Source Selection

The SSET evaluates each offeror's proposal and any subsequently submitted information or proposal revisions against the solicitation requirements and evaluation criteria. The Source Selection Evaluation Team (SSET) evaluates the offeror's understanding of the software task, the viability of the proposed approach, and the offeror's capability and capacity to perform. In addition, the SSET identifies and documents the strengths, deficiencies, uncertainties, weaknesses, and risks associated with each offeror's proposed approach.

During source selection, the SSET should typically accomplish the following software-related activities:

a. Review and evaluate the offeror's CS&S architecture, including all software to be developed, reused, and integrated, to ensure solicitation requirements can be satisfied.

b. Evaluate the completeness and soundness of the proposed technical approach to meeting computer systems and software requirements.

c. Evaluate for realism the size of the proposed software development and integration effort, considering expected software size growth during development, proposed software reuse, proposed modification to existing software, proposed use of COTS products, and other software development and integration risks.

d. Determine that the software size, technical content, development effort (cost), and schedule has been appropriately and consistently addressed throughout the proposal (for example, ensure the size of the software proposed in the technical volume is reflected in the cost volume).

e. Develop a conservative estimate of the required software development effort based on the proposed software size and development approach, and crosscheck this estimate:

    (1) If the SSET estimate shows that the proposed effort is not adequate, adjust the Most Probable Cost (MPC).

f. Develop a conservative estimate of the required software development schedule based on the proposed software size and development approach, and crosscheck this estimate:

    (1) Assess the software schedule risk in the context of the proposed IMS, including software-related IMS task durations, sequencing, and linkages.

    (2) If the SSET estimate shows that the proposed software development schedule is not adequate, provide inputs to a schedule risk assessment so that any resulting schedule extension can be dollarized and integrated into the MPC.

g. Evaluate the proposed software development and integration processes as defined in the proposed SDP.

    (1) Expect to see evidence of established processes in a company standard development approach, reflected in the program SDP.

    (2) Evaluate adequacy of and commitment to consistently apply the proposed processes through the SDP, IMP, IMS, and SOW. (Commitment to processes must be established from the beginning of the contract, across the development team. Required software activities and tasks should be clearly addressed and the temporal (sequential and concurrent) relationships of these activities should be clearly indicated. Event completion criteria should include relevant software engineering process steps. Engineering analysis should be performed to determine that the IMS reflects adequate time to apply the proposed software development processes.)

    (3) Evaluate the compatibility of the proposed software development processes with the proposed software effort, schedule, and performance baselines.

    (4) Evaluate the integration of software engineering within systems engineering.

h. Evaluate the proposed approach to identifying and managing computer system and software risks, and assess the initial risks and mitigation activities identified by the offerors.

i. Evaluate the proposed approach for software activity planning and statusing, including the use of software metrics.

j. Evaluate the proposed approach for software problem reporting, tracking, and resolution.

k. Evaluate the proposed approach for software sustainment planning.

l. Evaluate the block/incremental development approach, and ensure that adequate personnel, development stations, and integration labs are available to support any planned concurrent development.

m. Ensure that any proprietary rights or intellectual property issues are identified, and that appropriate rights are proposed based on the expected operational and support approaches for the software.

n. Ensure that offerors propose an adequate approach to testing/verifying GFS well prior to need, and that offerors understand such software is provided "as-is."

o. Evaluate the proposed approach to managing software suppliers, including flow-down of performance and process requirements, use of common development environments, balance of subcontract type and risk, and approach to insight, communication, and control.

3.4.3 Using Maturity Models to Evaluate Offeror Capability

The Software Engineering Institute's (SEI) Capability Maturity Model Integration (CMMI) is a widely adopted approach for process improvement, employed by numerous companies in countries around the world. It was developed using the earlier Capability Maturity Model (CMM) for software as a foundation. CMMI includes a model, which defines the goals, objectives, and expectations for processes in a number of process areas. It also includes an assessment method which can be used to rate how well the model is being applied in practice. Using the popular staged representation, process maturity is rated at one of five levels, where level one is basic, ad hoc management (see FIGURE 7). Level three is typically viewed as a minimum level of acceptable performance, where processes are defined and applied across a development organization. Levels four and five build on this foundation to include statistical process control and a continuous focus on improvement.

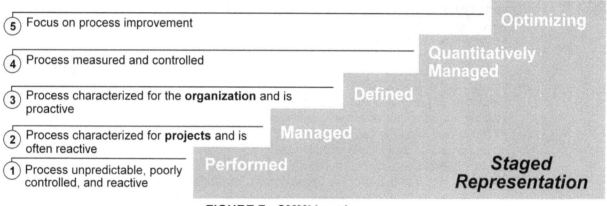

FIGURE 7. CMMI Levels.

There is sometimes a temptation for acquisition organizations to rely on CMMI ratings as a predictor of performance on actual development programs, and to simplify the evaluation of process capability during source selection by simply asking for and perhaps verifying CMMI results, or levels, during source selection. This is not good practice. The SEI provides the following cautions:

a. Levels are good indicators of *potential organizational performance.*

b. They describe how the next project *could perform* based on a sampling of existing projects.

c. Capability levels and maturity levels reside at the organizational level (corporation, major division) and are ***not** an indication of how any individual project is performing*.

There is no OSD or Air Force policy requiring that offerors/developers/contractors have a minimum maturity level (such as Level 3) to do business with the Government. Mark D. Schaeffer, OSD (AT&L), Systems and Software Engineering, stated the following in the July-August 2007 issue of Defense AT&L Magazine: "DoD does not place significant emphasis on

----

capability level or maturity level ratings, but rather promotes CMMI as a tool for internal process improvement. This lack of emphasis on ratings is prudent in the light of findings that not all suppliers are exhibiting behavior consistent with their attained CMMI maturity level rating."

Additionally, according to data collected and analyzed by the DCMA, there does not appear to be a link between maturity levels and program performance. Furthermore, there does not appear to be cost and schedule improvement by moving from Level 3 to Level 5 process maturity.

While CMMI has been shown to be a valuable tool for internal process improvement, it is clear that great care must be taken when trying to interpret and apply CMMI-related information in source selection. Acquisition organizations that have the resources, knowledge, and experience available to take a CMMI-based approach to evaluating offeror capability in the source selection timeframe should consider the following:

a. Do not assume that because the contractor asserts a specific maturity or capability level rating that they will execute that level of process proficiency on a new program. These ratings are at the business unit (or organizational unit) level and are not necessarily applicable to a specific program individually.

b. Unless the specific solicitation involves a program that is already in progress (e.g., a follow-on to a previous phase or a modification to an existing contract), using CMMI appraisals (Standard CMMI Appraisal Method for Process Improvement – SCAMPI) as part of the source selection process will provide little to no insight into how the contractor will perform on the next program. Typically, the contractor will not select, tailor, and execute process for the specific program until after it has been awarded.

c. Do not include requirements for any specific maturity or capability level ratings. Rather, include (in the SOW/CSOW) that the contractor is required to execute a minimum set of processes or process areas (PAs) that are important to the program. These PAs may include, for example, Requirements Development (RD), Requirements Management (REQM), Risk Management (RSKM), and Configuration Management (CM). Although it is recommended that simple statements of required maturity or capability levels be avoided, developers can be required to execute at least level 3 equivalent processes on the program. Note that process areas defined by CMMI as level 3 process areas are generally considered to encompass the key processes necessary for program execution. Disciplined process execution can be tied to award fee. If complete avoidance of any CMMI terminology is desirable, the minimum set of PAs to be implemented can be addressed in the SOW/CSOW.

d. Maturity or capability level performance information relative to the contractor business unit (or organizational unit) within which a specific program will reside may offer some insight into the source of the standard processes that may be implemented on that program. If this information is of interest, it can be requested in RFP Section L by requiring a full Appraisal Disclosure Statement (ADS) and Findings Briefing for any SCAMPIs that have been conducted on that business unit in the last three years. The ADS can identify and clarify relevant appraisal conditions and factors, and can provide some understanding that the process artifacts and tailoring procedures are available from which to draw for individual projects. Also, note that in general, valid, independent appraisal results will undergo quality checks and will be accepted by the SEI. Further, while provisions are made for "sensitive" data, if the results of the appraisal are to be announced publicly or used in a formal proposal, then the appraisal results must be placed on the SEI's Published Appraisal Results Site (PARS).

e. Past performance information can be useful in determining how well a contractor executed their standard processes and how well those processes benefited programs previously. However, the past performance questionnaire must be specifically tailored to expose this information in a useful manner.

f.   Language can be included in the contract (e.g., Section H clause) that allows the Government to conduct process reviews or appraisals at periodic points in the program at the Government's discretion. One or two of these reviews at key points in the program (e.g., post-IBR or pre-Critical Design Review (CDR)) will provide insight into how the contractor has tailored and implemented processes on the program. The notion that the Government will check on how processes are tailored and implemented is a strong motivator for the contractor to follow their processes after contract award.

3.4.4   *Sources of Additional Guidance*

a.   "*Choosing a Supplier: Due Diligence and CMMI*," News@SEI 2004 Number 3, CMMI in Focus, David M. Phillips.

b.   "*Understanding and Leveraging a Supplier's CMMI Efforts: A Guidebook for Acquirers*."

c.   *Air Force Federal Acquisition Regulation Supplement (AFFARS) Mandatory Procedure 5315.3 – Source Selection*

3.5 Applying Earned Value Management to Software

Earned value is an essential indicator of program health and serves as a powerful tool to gain insight into program status. EVM can and must be applied to manage and control software development.

In order to facilitate the implementation of EVM for software, the program office should:

a. Ensure the WBS is provided at the lowest level of tasks managed and includes appropriate critical software tasks and milestones tied to the EVM work package level. The objective is to establish a program WBS which mirrors the actual product(s) developed:

   (1) Typical WBS elements for software include the Software Specification Review (SSR), Preliminary Design, Preliminary Design Review (PDR), Detailed Design, Critical Design Review (CDR), Code & Unit Test, Integration Test, Software Qualification Test (SQT), System Test, and User/Field Test.

   (2) Place software elements in the WBS at appropriate levels which are consistent with the developed product architecture and hierarchy.

   (3) It is imperative that preliminary requirements be defined prior to establishing WBS estimates, since the Budgeted Cost of Work Scheduled (BCWS) for software cannot be determined without them.

b. Ensure that all software work is defined in work packages, and that the software work packages are managed and used as the basis for status reporting. This includes software work that may occur subsequent to software qualification, such as hardware/software integration and flight test.

c. Assess and understand the impacts or limitations of selected earned value reports such as the Contract Performance Report (CPR), and establish reporting requirements which facilitate the level of software insight desired.

   (1) If the software elements, appropriately placed in the WBS to reflect the to-be built product design, do not facilitate the desired identification and reporting of software status (e.g. system reporting at level 3 only and software elements are at lower levels), then the Contractor Data Requirements List (CDRL) should be tailored to include special reporting requirements to achieve the desired software earned value reporting. This special reporting could, for example, require collection and amalgamation of software earned value data from across the numerous WBS elements containing software for reporting as a single software report, or alternately, reporting of software earned value status could be required at the subsystem level to provide more detailed software insight.

   (2) It is important to establish reporting levels with enough granularity such that visibility into significant software development problems at the lower level components is not lost (washed out) in the reporting roll-up. Typical software reporting is done for subsystem design, code and test. For more granularity, track by candidates for change (e.g., Baseline Change Requests (BCRs)). For example, design for each BCR can be tracked as tasks to prepare for a common system or subsystem PDR and CDR.

   (3) It is important that the level of granularity be smaller than the reporting period. In other words, if EVM reports are examined monthly, then reported WBS elements

must be less than one month in duration to accurately portray progress. This eliminates "flat lined" EVM reports and unreliable EAC dates.

d. Ensure the program cost accounts and work packages reflect the WBS structure and are consistent with the software effort and schedule estimates for the program.

e. Ensure the work package schedules integrate into and are consistent with the program IMS and the working schedules used by developer's software managers.

f. Require the contractor to provide descriptions of how Earned Value (EV) is earned on software design, development, and test tasks. Develop an understanding of how the contractor earns value on these tasks (e.g., as a percentage of code size, as a percentage of test cases executed, 50% for starting a task and 50% for completing it), and how this impacts EV reporting.

g. Collect and review EV data to determine actual software effort and schedule status against the budgeted effort and schedule for the software components (schedule and cost variances). Status is determined by measuring technical progress and EV at the work package level.

h. Establish on-line collaborative (real-time or near-real-time) access to EV data to provide timely insight into software development status. Minimize the lag time between the end of an EV reporting period and the availability of EV analysis to more quickly identify problems or risks.

i. Use the software EV reporting to identify specific or systemic software development problem areas for focused monitoring or resolution, by identifying deviations and patterns of deviation from planned budget and schedule.

3.5.1   Sources of Additional Guidance

a. *OSD Guidance on Earned Value*: A web site that provides related policy and guidance, points of contact, frequently asked questions (FAQ), and other information on EVM.

b. *Defense Acquisition Guidebook*: Information specific to EVM.

3.6 Establishing and Managing Software Requirements

The purpose of establishing and managing requirements is to ensure that the requirements are analyzed, defined, complete, consistent, stable, and verifiable, consistent with the software development life cycle to be used.

Requirements identification, allocation, and verification are often a shared responsibility between the acquisition program office and the development contractor. The program office will normally focus on system level performance requirements identification and the contractor will focus on the lower level tiers (down to hardware/software or hardware/software sub-components) for which they are responsible.

System operators often have difficulty articulating exactly what they would like the system to do, especially from a Human Machine Interface (HMI) standpoint. Therefore, it is necessary for the acquisition program office and the development contractor to work with the operators to ensure that requirements as well as expectations and other constraints are well understood, and that the design approach will be acceptable. The product that results from this set of activities is a complete set of system requirements, including the HMI. The final system requirements are then decomposed into functionally allocated and derived "product" requirements that are used to guide the design and development of the product.

Interface requirements must be defined as appropriate between components of the software system, and to external software and hardware as necessary. Requirements for interfaces are typically defined in terms of overall functionality, including such items as: origination, destination, stimulus, response, data characteristics, timing, and electrical and mechanical characteristics.

Requirements, at any level must be complete, consistent, and traceable to applicable higher level (e.g. system and subsystem) requirements and lower level (e.g. subsystem and software) design and implementation, and must also be traceable to the verification methodology.

Modern acquisition and evolutionary development approaches allow for the gradual maturation of requirements at the system level. However, once the development of a particular block/increment of capability is started, any change to the block/increment requirements will impact the near term product. If such late changes are allowed, some level of rework will be required and the software will likely be late and over budget.

3.6.1 Requirements Basics

Establishment and management of requirements includes the following steps, described here without regard to how those specific steps are allocated between program office and contractor:

a. Assess each top-level requirement for feasibility of implementation, consistency within program constraints, and its ability to be verified. If the requirement is impossible to implement within cost and schedule constraints, it must be identified as an issue and resolved by adjusting budget, relaxing schedule, and changing or eliminating the requirement.

b. Use functional or object-oriented analysis to define a functional architecture that can be used as a basis for allocating requirements.

c. Allocate all system, subsystem, and interface requirements to appropriate hardware and software configuration items. Ensure each requirement:

(1) Is written as a single definitive statement.

(2) Has a unique identification number for tracking purposes.

      (3)   Can be traced to a higher level source requirement or analysis (if a derived requirement).

      (4)   Has been allocated to a specific Computer Software Configuration Item (CSCI).

d.   Ensure that each performance requirement has one or more corresponding verification requirements. Involve those who will perform testing activities to ensure that requirements are testable. The specification section 4 verification requirement should define a means of objective measurement. (Note: this goes beyond identifying the category and method of verification in the section 4 verification matrix. This is not intended to be a set of test procedures but rather a short statement of the method and conditions for demonstrating the requirement has been satisfied. This benefits the program by establishing a set of test requirements upon which to build a test plan and forcing ambiguity out of the section 3 performance requirements.)

e.   Identify analyses, trade studies, prototyping, and demonstration efforts for risk reduction, considering the following:

      (1)   Completeness: Are all higher level requirements allocated?

      (2)   Consistency: Is the content, format, and notation from requirement to requirement, and specification to specification similar?

      (3)   Feasibility: Can the requirement be met?

      (4)   Balance: What are the trade-offs between requirements? (Optimization on specific requirements can lead to less than optimal system performance—optimization of the system is the goal.)

      (5)   Verifiability/testability: Can the requirement be objectively verified?

      (6)   Human factors: Is the design consistent with sound human factors principles?

f.   Complete the definition of derived software requirements and examine them for consistency with system requirements, feasibility, and the effects of various implementation strategies. Monitor derived requirements size volatility since derived requirements are often a significant source of software size growth.

g.   Apply early aggressive activities to verify that software intended for reuse fits the following criteria:

      (1)   The advertised performance of the software to be reused satisfies performance requirements.

      (2)   The software to be reused exists and is available.

      (3)   The actual performance of the software to be reused satisfies performance requirements and does not have inherent shortfalls that will lead to additional growth.

      (4)   There is a plan to address future upgrades/support of the reused software.

h.   Ensure developers flow top level requirements down to lower level specifications and to lower tier suppliers, including software configuration item specifications.

i.   Verify CSCI-to-CSCI and CSCI-to-Hardware Critical Item (HWCI) interface requirements identification and definition.

j. Verify that an adequate and compatible set of tools are in place to capture multi-level requirements (systems down through software) and design evolution.

k. Use operational scenarios to the extent possible to demonstrate, or bring to life, what the requirements are trying to capture. (Operational scenarios portray the product, end user, and other entities in the intended environment, and are a useful tool for discovering and refining requirements.)

l. Use a requirements management tool (such as DOORS, Clear Case, or RTM) to provide:

    (1) Unique identification of each requirement by number.

    (2) A means to capture allocation of high level requirements to lower level systems, subsystems, and components.

    (3) Traceability of requirements vertically (from the highest level to the lowest level) and horizontally (by various threads) to ensure full requirements coverage (Traceability also helps to identify areas of the software/hardware impacted by a change, determine the testability of the software/hardware, identify the scope of coverage for all levels of testing, and define coupling of functional threads throughout the software/system mechanization, including identification of requirements that support safety critical functions.)

3.6.2 Requirements and Incremental Software Development

Incremental software development is an approach that allows complex systems to be built via several increments delivered over time. Incremental development reduces risk in developing the total capability, facilitates the development of basic capability first, allows verification of basic capabilities prior to developing more complex features, accommodates design refinement, and with sufficient staff, can shorten the overall development timeline to initial operational capability. Incremental development is now the norm for complex software systems.

In an incremental development environment, requirements will naturally evolve. There is an inherent give-and-take between requirements, designs, and operational scenarios. As designs are selected to implement certain requirements, or operational scenarios change, software requirements may have to be revised or refined. And requirements changes may ripple from one level to another, such as from software components to the overall software system.

In addition to having adequate staff and other development resources, the key to incremental development is to properly manage the associated requirements. Incremental requirements definition has not worked well on some past programs. Proceeding into design and implementation for a block/increment of specific development activity with incomplete requirements is a high risk approach, particularly in unprecedented software development.

In order to best ensure success with incremental software development, the following should be considered:

a. Complete the software and interface requirements specifications and baseline them prior to developing incremental software builds.

b. Map/allocate the requirements into all planned builds. Failure to do so will increase the likelihood that functionality will migrate to later builds, the initial delivery will not meet user expectations, unplanned builds will become necessary, and the delivery of full functionality will be delayed.

c. In any approach that involves concurrent development of two or more increments:

(1) Ensure adequate resources (personnel, development/integration labs) are in place.

(2) Ensure there are adequate controls to prevent diverging baselines and the associated program impact (rework, schedule delays).

3.6.3   Software Size Control

Design understanding and evolution is an inherent part of the development process for complex systems. As each level of requirements and design is developed and understood, a better picture of the supporting requirements and design for subcomponents evolves. For systems implemented in software, this process often results in software size growth due to additional decomposed and derived requirements at the lower system tiers. Decomposed requirements trace to higher level requirements documents, while derived requirements trace to design decisions or results of analyses. A typical challenge for embedded systems is that software size often grows "under the radar," unconstrained, unmanaged, and unattended as if it were for free with no adverse program baseline impact. In order to combat this situation, consider establishing a software size control program.

The objectives of software size control are to:

a. Prevent uncontrolled growth in the amount of software that must be developed.

b. Validate that newly defined derived requirements which are driving software growth are, in fact, necessary to meet overall system performance requirements.

c. Avoid related growth in the requirement for computer processing resources.

d. Prevent adverse impact on program schedule and resources.

e. Provide a context for making decisions on corrective actions by understanding the impact of software change on cost, schedule, performance, and quality.

Ensure the contractor implements software change management by establishing a process to control baselines. The process should begin by utilizing the proposal baselines from source selection, or software size estimates otherwise available at the start of a project.

Ensure the contractor considers the following in managing software growth:

a. Formal size estimating methods, based on actuals from the developer's experience.

b. Integration with the system/software/hardware engineering process.

c. Rigorous software size baseline control.

(1) Control requirements creep.

(2) Establish a verification requirement for each performance requirement at the time the performance requirement is written.

(3) Use formal Engineering Change Proposals (ECPs) with adjustment to cost and schedule.

(4) Defer "growth" requirements to a follow-on release.

d. Process to eliminate software functionality which is not essential to meeting requirements.

(1) Beware of design decisions that adversely affect planned reuse.

e. Working groups or control boards responsible to manage requirements and to monitor derived requirements volatility.

f. System/software architecture designed to accommodate growth.

g. Prototypes or demonstrations of unprecedented, high risk areas.

h. Incentives for software size containment.

3.7   Acquisition Insight and Involvement

Program offices must maintain continuous insight into software design, development, and verification activities via metrics, formal technical review meetings, and other less formal means of communications. Armed with this insight, a program can measure performance, proactively manage risks, and address problems which inevitably arise during acquisition.

3.7.1   Software Metrics

Software metrics should be an integral part of a software developer's standard processes. Program offices should gain insight into proposed metrics during source selection, and developers should commit to the consistent use of those metrics, including collecting, analyzing, and reporting. Software metrics should:

    a. Be integral to the developer's processes.

    b. Clearly portray variances between planned and actual performance.

    c. Provide early detection or prediction of situations that require management attention.

    d. Support the assessment of the impact of proposed changes on the program.

In SAF/AQ/US Memorandum 04A-003, "Revitalizing the Software Aspects of Systems Engineering," (20 September 2004), the Air Force has defined the following core software metrics:

    a. Software size.

    b. Software development effort.

    c. Software development schedule.

    d. Software defects.

    e. Software requirements definition and stability.

    f. Software development staffing.

    g. Software progress (design, coding, and testing).

    h. Computer resources utilization.

Additional guidance on these Air Force core software metrics is provided in Appendix H.

In addition to the core metrics, program offices and developers should consider, mutually agree on, and periodically (as needed) implement additional metrics or methods of insight to address software issues deemed critical or unique to the program.

Useful information on implementation of software metrics is available from the following sources:

    a. Practical Software and Systems Measurement (PSM): PSM is a DoD sponsored activity developed to meet today's software and system technical and management challenges. It is an information-driven measurement process that addresses the unique technical and business goals of an organization. The guidance in PSM represents best practices used by measurement professionals within the software and system acquisition and engineering communities.

b. Software Engineering Institute (SEI): The SEI offers an array of courses, presentations, and publications related to software metrics and measurement. Two items of note include:

(1) Software Engineering Measurement and Analysis (SEMA) initiative. SEMA is intended to help organizations develop and evolve useful measurement and analysis practices.

(2) Goal-Driven Software Measurement. This SEI Guidebook provides an in-depth discussion on selecting and developing software measures in support of business goals.

c. Guidelines for Successful Acquisition and Management of Software-Intensive Systems: Chapter eight of this guidebook, published by the Software Technology Support Center, provides good recommendations for establishing a metrics program.

d. DoD Data Analysis Center for Software (DACS) Gold Practices (requires on-line registration with DACS to access their documents):

(1) Metrics-Based Scheduling: Establish realistic software development or maintenance schedules based on accurate estimates of software size and effort.

(2) Binary Quality Gates: Defines completion criteria for each low level task, assesses the adequacy and completeness of the finished process, and tracks completion at the binary level (done or not done). This practice addresses the problem referred to as the "80% syndrome," when programs seem to stall near completion.

Regardless of the metrics chosen for use, they should be defined in the SDP, and should be tailored and implemented consistent with Air Force requirements and the developer's internal tools and processes. As a minimum, the program office and contractor must agree on how the information will be made available. There should also be agreement on the specific data to be collected/reported, the requirement for flowdown/rollup regarding any subcontractors, and the frequency of reporting. Program offices should have continuous on-line access to current metrics and other appropriate program management information, and this access should be a contract requirement.

3.7.2 Qualitative Indicators

Gathering and evaluating metrics and earned value data provides program quantitative information and can promote a collaborative environment between the program office and contractor. Obtaining qualitative insight into the program is also important, and a primary source of qualitative insight is involvement in program reviews. Qualitative data can be an early indicator of progress, or an "early warning" of emerging problems that can be addressed in a timely manner, and avoided or mitigated with an effective corrective action plan. The program office and contractor should scrutinize any discrepancies between qualitative and quantitative indicators and determine the reasons for the differences.

See Appendix A, "Software in the Integrated Master Plan," and Appendix F, "Computer Systems and Software Criteria for Technical Reviews," for more information on software-related content in technical reviews.

Additional opportunities for obtaining qualitative insight include:

a. Participating in early program acquisition strategy sessions and solicitation preparation activities.

b. Participating in Integrated Baseline Reviews. These reviews can be used to gain insight into the software task planning activities including inchstones for CSCI and component development as well as work package closure criteria (potential qualitative indicator). This information has a direct relationship to EVM in that it shows how the developer "takes credit" for activities and product development completed. Issues arising in the review can be addressed in follow-on technical reviews.

c. Monitoring ongoing work to determine: progress against planned work; requirements changes and derived requirements evolution; changes in software size; problem report status, trends, and criticality.

d. Ensuring contractually required performance reports provide the information needed to evaluate developers' efforts, consistent with the software content in the IMP, IMS, and WBS. See section 3.5 for additional information.

3.7.3   Involvement in Development Activities

The program office should define the role and activities of program office personnel in the detailed software development activities. This includes, for example, the program office role and level of involvement in:

a. Level of access to software products and involvement in review and approval.

b. Approval of software requirements specifications and test procedures.

c. Detailed design activities such as peer reviews and technical reviews.

d. Witnessing of lab integration/test and formal test activities.

e. Monitoring and reviewing in-place development processes, comparing with SDP requirements, and recommending improvements.

f. Configuration control of development and product specifications and design documents.

g. Monitoring and disposition of defect/problem reports, especially for critical software problems[1].

h. Determination of fitness for intended use of software products.

Program office personnel should contractually define their planned interactions with the developer, to the extent possible. They should also plan and coordinate their activities with those on-site DCMA personnel, when available, to ensure they maintain the proper level of insight and involvement into developer activities without interfering with the developer's responsibilities.

3.7.4   Software Resources Data Report

The Software Resources Data Report (SRDR) is used to obtain both the estimated and actual characteristics of new software developments or upgrades. However, unlike the other topics addressed in this section, SRDRs are *not* intended as a tool to provide program level insight into

---

[1] Critical software problems (summarized from previous DoD and MIL software standards):
- Jeopardize safety, security, or other critical requirements
- Prevent the accomplishment of an essential capability
- Adversely affect the accomplishment of an essential capability, and no work-around solution is known
- Adversely affect technical, cost, or schedule risks to the project or life cycle support of the system, and no work-around solution is known

software development progress. The purpose of SRDR data collection is to improve DoD's ability to estimate the costs of software intensive programs.

SRDRs are required for any activity developing/producing software elements within Acquisition Category (ACAT) IA, ACAT IC and ACAT ID programs, regardless of contract type, for any element with a projected effort greater than $25M. The data collection and reporting applies to developments and upgrades whether performed under a commercial contract or internally by a Government Central Design Activity (CDA). While the SRDR data item description contains mandatory data items that must be reported, the data is tailorable to align with the reporting contractor's internal accounting and metrics systems. The contractor is also permitted to deliver the data in the format deemed most efficient and expedient.

The SRDR reporting threshold is based upon a broad definition of "software development." The following guidelines are used:

a. The software development effort of the prime contract, along with the software development efforts of all sub-contracts under the prime are considered.

b. All increments (or builds, releases, and so on) that will be developed and delivered under the contract are considered.

c. All software components (or segments, or CSCIs, or elements, and so on) developed and delivered by either the prime contractor or sub-contractors are considered. This can include mission system software components, training simulator software, modeling and simulation software, mission planning software, and other mission or support software developed and ultimately delivered.

d. All software development activities that are associated with software development and typically estimated by Government cost analysts are considered. This means not only are core development activities like design, and code & unit test included, but so are activities such as requirements analysis, software architecture, software and system/software integration, qualification or acceptance testing, software program management, software quality assurance, and software configuration management.

Each SRDR consists of two parts - the actual data being reported and an associated data dictionary. The reported data addresses software context, size, schedule, effort, and quality. The data dictionary defines each of the data elements used in the report and describes the methods and rules used to perform the data measurement or estimation. The data dictionary also contains the details necessary to allow Government analysts to correctly interpret the responses.

The Government program office must submit an SRDR Initial Government Report with their initial submission of the Cost Analysis Requirements Description (CARD). Reporting requirements for developer SRDRs should be implemented contractually, and prime contractors must flow down the reporting requirements for SRDRs to all sub-contractors meeting the reporting threshold. Developers must generally submit an Initial Developer Report within 60 days of contract award and a Final Developer Report within 60 days of contract completion. Additionally, for each software release, developers must submit an Initial Developer Report within 60 days of the release start and a Final Developer Report within 60 days of the release completion.

The project office may tailor the submission deadlines, as appropriate, for exceptionally small or large software efforts. Also, the program office may choose to combine a set of smaller releases within a contract into a single release for reporting purposes. Separate software element developments within a single contract may be reported separately or, at the discretion of the Government, may be aggregated. Data for subcontracts of less than $25M in software development may also be aggregated into one or more reports. Software development subcontracts for more than $25M are to be reported to the Government separately by the subcontractor.

3.7.5   Sources of Additional Guidance for SRDR

    a.   <u>Introduction to SRDR</u>

    b.   <u>CSDR Planning Forms and Instructions</u>

    c.   <u>Cost and Software Data Reporting Manual</u> (<u>DoD 5000.04-M-1</u>, 18 April 2007)

    d.   <u>Initial Government Report and Data Dictionary</u>

    e.   <u>Initial Developer Report</u>

    f.   <u>Final Developer Report</u>

    g.   <u>CSDR Reporting Plan</u>

    h.   <u>CSDR Contracting Information</u>

3.8 Safety Critical Systems

Development of safety-critical systems requires discipline, diligence, and oversight in the system and software development process (reviews, code inspections, test coverage analysis). It is imperative to address the hardware, software, and computer system architecture in an integrated manner. Safety critical systems must continue to provide service in the presence of failures and therefore the design must incorporate redundancy and fault tolerant techniques. The development and test processes for safety-critical systems must not be compromised even in the face of schedule and budget pressures.

A Safety Critical Function (SCF) is a top-level function whose loss could potentially result in loss of the system (air vehicle, missile) and/or life. A SCF thread is the combination of safety critical elements/components (software, computers, interfaces, sensors and effectors, inputs and outputs) whose overall contribution supports a given safety critical function. SCF threads uniquely trace the mechanization of each safety critical function throughout the system, identifying the thread weaknesses (single path, single sensor input, and lack of required redundancy) for paths through the software, hardware, and computer system/system architecture. The same hardware, computer systems, and buses can be within multiple SCF threads.

The safety-critical developmental process is characterized by addressing the integrated system; ensuring the system architecture is robust; tracing functional threads (including SCFs) through the system architecture; ensuring vertical and horizontal design mechanization is well understood; and ensuring test coverage is complete.

SCF testing includes the software low-level testing, full qualification of all requirements, functional thread mechanization verification, and extensive System Integration Lab (SIL) testing, with comprehensive failure insertion testing performed at all levels. Software qualification is often considered complete at the completion of software level testing of Software Requirements Specification (SRS) requirements. However, for safety-critical systems, testing of software functionality cannot be considered complete until system level lab testing or testing on the actual system has been completed. For aircraft this would include performing on-air vehicle tests, and when appropriate, low speed and high speed taxi tests. Continuing with the aircraft example, the airworthiness certification process, as detailed in MIL-HDBK-516B, sets very specific requirements for safety-critical computer systems and software.

It is imperative to implement a system safety program per MIL-STD-882 in conjunction with a SCF analysis to determine the criticality level required for the associated architecture trade studies and processes to follow. Increased discipline in process requirements for design, development, integration, requirements traceability, and more exhaustive testing increases upfront costs and schedule. However, this up-front attention to developing a robust safety critical system results in minimal operational system problems and improved rework cost savings later in the program, far out-weighing the upfront costs.

Exhaustive testing for safety critical systems should be automated wherever possible. The automation facilitates test repeatability and results in significant future reductions in turn-around time for releasing software/system updates while mitigating technical risk.

Programs should take the following actions in the development of safety-critical systems:

a. Identify the safety critical functions and understand the implications to the architecture, system, subsystems, hardware, and software through the system level safety analysis.

b. Perform architecture analysis/trade studies to define and understand the capability of the architecture for worst case loading and full functional capability (note that a best practice is to avoid using more than 90% of the throughput of any single processor, or 90% of the entire system throughput, in a safety critical application).

c. Determine the developers' capability, capacity, and experience to develop, integrate, and test safety critical system architectures and software.

d. Ensure Failure Modes and Effects Analysis (FMEA) is performed at all system and component levels (including hardware and software) to address potential failure scenarios.

e. Ensure safety critical requirements at all system and component levels are baselined early in the development phase and tracked throughout the development.

f. Validate performance of planned software reuse and COTS products in safety critical systems.

g. Establish an effective means for mitigating safety risks through system design and development.

h. Develop extensive Failure Modes Effects Testing (FMET) test cases tied to the FMEA at all levels of testing.

i. Establish a software test process which accounts for testing of all requirements and functional threads at all structural levels up through the system level to form a software qualification baseline (note this baseline means full qualification and does not take credit for delta qualifications for safety-critical functions).

j. Develop and perform thorough tests of the safety-critical hardware and software components.

k. Develop and properly apply core and regression test processes at the system level for all incremental releases from an established baseline.

l. Develop and follow a certification process appropriate to the domain.

m. Ensure vertical requirements traceability from system level requirements to the lowest requirements level for the system to design, code, test cases, and test procedures.

n. Ensure functional thread traceability throughout the software by tracing software/hardware requirements required to support safety critical functions to design, code, test cases and test procedures.

o. Ensure Failure Modes, and Effects, Criticality Analysis (FMECA) is performed at all levels to analyze hardware reliability.

p. Develop and sustain high-fidelity SILs that duplicate the actual target system hardware, software, and interfaces so that representative tests can be conducted and failures can be detected and diagnosed.

q. Plan for substantial testing in the SILs to verify the software requirements, performance, and safety of the software/system.

r. Develop and follow a process for incorporating necessary hardware and software changes into the computer system architecture with minimal impact to safe operation.

s. Ensure proper engineering involvement is maintained in all decisions regarding documentation, maintenance, and operational procedures for safety-critical systems for the entire development and operations/support lifetime of the system.

3.8.1   *Sources of Additional Guidance*

   a.   Appendix G, "Process considerations for Safety-Critical Systems."

3.9 Non-Developmental Software

DoD and the Air Force encourage the use of NDS. NDS is any software that is not legacy software for the program, or is not developed as part of the effort being accomplished by the developer team. NDS includes COTS software, GFS, Open Source Software (OSS), and software being reused from another program. NDS can provide significant benefits including faster delivery of capabilities, reduced costs, and faster technology upgrades. NDS can also introduce numerous risks to the program that can have contractual and long-term sustainment implications. Developers must understand when they use NDS they are responsible to ensure the NDS is properly analyzed, tested, and integrated into the system so that program performance requirements are fully satisfied.

3.9.1 General Considerations for NDS

Robust systems engineering is essential for developing a system using NDS. Systems and software engineering processes must be tailored for NDS-based development. Evaluations must be performed to identify potential NDS solutions and to ensure a complete understanding of the benefits and potential impacts. There must be a full life cycle understanding including maintenance costs, warranty and licensing costs, update requirements, and any other considerations which impact the system life cycle. Any required long-term support from the original NDS developer must be planned for. The fit and integration of NDS into the system must be considered. Since NDS may contain defects known or unknown to the original developer, the program team must understand the significance of those defects; how/when such defects will be fixed; and whether, how, and when the updated/corrected NDS will be incorporated into the system. This is a significant issue since it has been observed that COTS products average new releases every ten months, and are typically no longer supported after three releases. These timeframes are short compared to the operational life of many Air Force embedded systems.

The use of COTS brings additional challenges. Be aware that feature and functionality sets for COTS products are market-driven. Control of the future direction of the component is surrendered. Modifying COTS software is strongly discouraged, as the resulting component is no longer a COTS product. Programs have had significant difficulties resulting from ill-considered decisions to modify COTS. Also, although security and assurance are important considerations for all software activities, they are critical for COTS products, which may have been developed outside the normal trusted supplier base that is subject to industrial security requirements. COTS products must undergo a security risk assessment commensurate with the system's requirements and vulnerabilities.

When contemplating the use of NDS software, consider the following:

a. Ensure decisions to use NDS are based on and are traceable to validated system architecture and design requirements.

b. Include appropriate NDS activities in the program IMP/IMS.

c. Evaluate all proposed NDS to the extent possible at the start of the development (refer to the factors and attributes described in section 3.2, "Estimating Software Size, Effort, and Schedule," and note that there can be a high level of uncertainty early in the development).

d. Establish configuration control procedures to address NDS integration, upgrades, and changes throughout the system life cycle.

e. Assess suitability and manage technical risk inherent in NDS during the system development phase. Identify and manage risks associated with:

(1) Modifying NDS to meet program needs.

(2) Availability of supplier support to fix critical problems in a timely manner.

(3) The program approach to implementing new NDS versions when the original developer decides to fix problems or otherwise upgrade the product.

(4) Unavailability of NDS when needed.

(5) Limited or no access to source code (locking into a vendor for life cycle support).

(6) Rights to modify the source code.

f. Develop and implement an appropriate test and evaluation strategy for NDS.

g. Implement the necessary contractual clauses to address NDS issues such as licensing, data rights, and warranty/support.

h. Address security/assurance concerns with COTS software:

(1) Be aware of vulnerabilities. Review reports of known problems ("bug lists") usually published by the COTS developer.

(2) Review security advisories published by organizations such as the Computer Emergency Response Team Coordination Center (CERT/CC) at Carnegie Mellon University.

(3) Determine compliance with open standards, such as Transmission Control Protocol/Internet Protocol (TCP/IP) and Common Object Request Broker Architecture (CORBA), to understand how the COTS interacts with other components.

(4) Ensure the software developer/integrator understands how the selected COTS works and interfaces with the rest of the system.

(5) Develop and implement a system/software architecture that accommodates any residual risk from NDS/COTS components.

i. Plan, during system development, for NDS technology refresh and Post Deployment Software Support (PDSS). Planning should address responsibilities, milestones, projected update phases and cycles, budgets and schedules, and managing emergency updates.

3.9.2 *Government Furnished Software*

Special considerations apply when GFS is incorporated into an embedded system. All of the benefits and risks from other NDS apply, and additionally:

a. An Associate Contractor Agreement (ACA) between the embedded system developer and the original developer of the GFS may be appropriate to ensure rapid, clear, and concise communication.

b. The program office should consider codifying a government-to-government relationship (memorandum of agreement (MOA), other agreements) with the original acquiring organization to outline roles, responsibilities, and agreements.

----

c. The program office and contractor should codify the roles, responsibilities, and performance expectations related to the GFS. Contractor responsibilities and expectations related to GFS should be clearly understood.

d. The development contract should be structured to ensure the Government is not held responsible for the performance or support of the GFS. Refer to Appendix E, "Software Contracting Considerations."

3.9.3   Open Source Software

Open Source Software (OSS), sometimes referred to as Free and Open Source Software (FOSS), is computer software that includes source code that can be used and modified by the user without paying licensing fees or royalties. OSS is not public domain software or freeware. It is copyrighted and includes a license agreement restricting its use, modification, and distribution.

The Open Source Initiative (OSI) contains more information on open source and open source licenses. The OSI is a non-profit corporation which maintains the complete Open Source Definition consisting of ten requirements which software must meet to be considered open source, and the OSI license review process which, through a public review process, ensures that licenses and software labeled as "open source" comply with the Open Source Definition and conform to existing community norms and expectations.

Potential benefits of OSS include better quality, higher reliability, more flexibility, lower cost, and not being locked into a single vendor. Programs should proceed cautiously however, since there is very limited experience to date in applying open source in DoD embedded systems. Concerns about possible security risks are often raised about OSS because its source code is freely available and may be modified by anyone. However, closed or proprietary software is often hacked and security vulnerabilities are regularly exposed. Studies appear to indicate that OSS is no more or no less susceptible to security or reliability issues. A program sponsored by the Department of Homeland Security reported (Open Source Report 2008) that the typical piece of OSS contains a security vulnerability for each 1000 lines of code – comparable to average commercial software.

DoD and Air Force have established as a priority developing policy and guidance to leverage the benefits of Open Technology Development (OTD) and OSS. The DoD OTD Roadmap (April 2006) states: "DoD needs to use open technology design and development methodologies to increase the speed at which military systems are delivered to the warfighter, and accelerate the development of new, adaptive capabilities that leverage DoD's massive investments in software infrastructure." SAF/AQ and SAF/XC jointly signed a memo on 20 December 2007 ("Implementation of OTD") which defines specific action to incentivize (not mandate) the adoption of OTD and OSS in Air Force acquisition programs and systems.

DoD policy treats OSS in a manner similar to COTS software. As with any COTS solution, the use of OSS must adhere to all Federal, DoD, and Air Force policies and be based on open standards to support DoD's goals of net-centricity and interoperability.

Users of OSS need to understand, and ensure compliance with the license for the OSS product they plan to use. There are many types of OSS licenses, and each has different terms and conditions. These licensing requirements may be complex, so consultation with legal counsel is recommended.

OSS license requirements may include making the source code available, publishing a copyright notice, placing a disclaimer of warranty on distributed copies, and giving any recipient of the program a copy of the license. Some OSS licenses, such as the GNU General Public License (GPL), allow users to copy, modify and distribute the OSS, but the source code of the entire system which incorporated that OSS product must be, in turn, treated as OSS, subject to the terms and conditions of the GPL. The Linux operating system is an example of OSS used in DoD that is licensed under the GPL. Other OSS licenses are similar to the GPL, but only the module or component that incorporated the OSS product becomes OSS.

Just as for any COTS software, organizations acquiring, using or developing OSS must ensure that it is configured in accordance with DoD and Air Force security guidance. The potential benefits of OSS make it a valid option. However, these benefits must be carefully weighed against DoD specific security requirements. The Information Assurance Support Environment (IASE) provides the most current information on DoD Information Assurance (IA) requirements.

The Air Force IA Community of Practice (CoP) listing provides additional sources of Air Force specific guidance.

3.10 Software Assurance and Anti-Tamper Protection

For decades, organizations have strived to develop affordable, secure, trustworthy software. Despite significant strides toward this goal, there is ample evidence that adversaries retain their ability to compromise systems. Adversaries have a broad arsenal that includes:

    a. Insider attacks.

    b. Social engineering attacks.

    c. Physical attacks.

    d. Attacks on the global supply chain.

    e. Cyber attacks.

These attacks are often very hard to prevent or even detect. Consequently, there is growing awareness that software must be designed, built, and operated with the expectation that system components will have unknown vulnerabilities. Systems must continue to meet (possibly degraded) functionality, performance, and security goals despite these vulnerabilities. Vulnerabilities should be addressed through a comprehensive lifecycle approach. Software assurance is obtained by utilizing specific technologies and processes to reduce these vulnerabilities. While the steps outlined below are significant, this Air Force approach is the minimum required to provide AT protection and comply with DoD Software Assurance (SWA) requirements.

3.10.1 Software Assurance

Software Assurance is the justified confidence that the software functions as intended and is free of exploitable vulnerabilities, either intentionally or unintentionally designed or inserted as part of the system at any time during the lifecycle. These measures of confidence are achieved by SWA Activities. These are a planned, systematic set of multi-disciplinary activities which are used to achieve the acceptable measures of SWA and manage the risk of exploitable vulnerabilities. These activities, which should be tailored based on the criticality of the software (Critical Program Information (CPI) and Critical Technology (CT)) include:

    a. Ensuring SWA related system architecture, design, and development activities required of the developer are addressed in the acquisition documents (SOW, specifications, test plans), including:

        (1) Evaluating software developer contractor team SWA risks.

        (2) Ensuring personnel security clearance.

        (3) Securing the development environment.

        (4) Evaluating the contractor team's software development out-sourcing policy.

        (5) Identifying system critical COTS software source code pedigree and risk.

        (6) Providing repeatable trusted development activities encompassing the complete lifecycle of the system.

        (7) Incorporating software (SW) vulnerability analysis tools and training.

        (8) Ensuring that code changes are assessed to determine the impact on the overall system security posture.

b. Ensuring the system has obtained Information Assurance (IA) approval, including:

   (1) Reviewing program security policy and Concept of Operations (CONOPS) for specific IA requirements.

   (2) Performing the IA threat and vulnerability assessment.

   (3) Identifying appropriate IA requirements and integrating them into the SRD.

   (4) Developing test procedures and test plans.

   (5) Performing the IA risk assessment and mitigation plan.

c. Identifying COTS software components and determining IA risks before and after integration, including:

   (1) Ensuring COTS software supplier assurance.

   (2) Ensuring IA or IA enabled COTS software (security guards, operating system, firewalls) comply with National Security Telecommunications and Information Systems Security Policy (NSTISSP) No. 11, July 03.

   (3) Ensuring all embedded crypto-systems are National Security Agency/National Information Assurance Partnership (NSA/NIAP) validated.

d. Recommending a SWA risk mitigation approach and/or reaching agreement with the user on the level of SWA risk the user is willing to accept.

3.10.2 Anti-Tamper Protection

Anti Tamper (AT) prevents the reverse engineering and exploitation of military critical software technologies (e.g. algorithm, code segment, a software system as defined by DoDD 5200.39, Technology Protection) in order to deter technology transfer, alteration of system capability, or the development of countermeasures to U.S. systems. AT is an emerging umbrella term that covers the process, activities, and materiel implementation(s) to protect U.S. military and business technology from compromise when that technology is associated with or made vulnerable to reverse engineering through Foreign Military Sales (FMS), Direct Commercial Sales (DCS), worldwide operations. The following steps are required by DoD policy and Milestone B criteria to establish software AT protection:

a. Identify potential software related critical technologies (CT) requiring AT (as defined in DoDD 5200.39-R).

b. Identify threats to the software.

c. Identify vulnerabilities.

d. Identify attack scenarios.

e. Identify impacts if exploited.

f. Identify exploitation timelines to minimize impacts.

g. Perform risk analysis.

h. Select from potential critical technologies those that must be protected.

i. Identify the available potential AT techniques for each critical technology.

j.   Select potential implementations and perform risk assessment with each technique.

k.   Down-select to recommended protection solution.

l.   Develop the final AT plan and obtain AT plan approval.

3.11 Configuration Management

Configuration Management (CM) is a process for controlling system products, processes, and related documentation. The CM effort includes identifying, documenting, and verifying the functional and physical characteristics of an item; recording the configuration of an item; and controlling changes to an item and its documentation. CM provides a complete audit trail of decisions and design modifications as it establishes and maintains consistency and traceability of a product's performance, functional, and physical attributes with its requirements, design, and operational information throughout the product life cycle. Software CM should be conducted using best practices considering guidance provided in MIL-HDBK-61A, Configuration Management Guidance, EIA-649 "National Consensus Standard for Configuration Management," and ISO 12207 "Standard for Information Technology - Software Life Cycle Processes" (and subsets). In addition, paragraph E1.1.16 of DoDD 5000.01 states that acquisition managers shall consider factors that best support implementing performance-based strategies throughout the product life cycle, when making CM decisions.

Program office CM processes should ensure configuration management activities are accomplished throughout the acquisition lifecycle. The delegation of CM responsibilities will be determined by the System Program Manager/Program Manager (SPM/PM) and reflected in the contract. A key aspect of CM activities for software is to capture the declared configuration item (CI) baseline (e.g., Computer Program Configuration Items (CPCIs) and CSCIs), in order to ensure no unauthorized changes are made to the baseline and all authorized changes are tracked. The unique identification of the configuration items provides the PM with appropriate visibility to manage and control cost, schedule, and performance for software products.

CM processes should:

a. Establish and maintain a Configuration Management Plan (CMP) that includes processes for the identification, requirement traceability, change management, status accounting, and verification for controlling configuration items, components, software tools, software laboratories, and deliverable work products.

   (1) Establish a change management process, including processes to identify: proposed changes, tracking procedures, data required for evaluation, configuration change board processes, and implementation procedures for approving changes and updating technical data.

   (2) Identify the change approval authority and change board membership by function.

   (3) Control configuration items and supporting documentation changes to the baselines.

   (4) Establish SDR and software tracking metrics.

   (5) Establish/identify quality control (QC) criteria and guidance.

   (6) Identify software development guidance (e.g., SDP).

      (a) Define defect/deficiency reporting and tracking processes.

      (b) Identify/define the CM aspects of review processes and procedures (i.e., peer reviews, design reviews).

b. Ensure the developer selects a CM toolset that addresses the CM needs, including the ability to manage multiple baselines, both before and after formal release. The toolset should provide and/or address:

    (1) Version control capabilities for pre/post-release code, documentation, and tools, including:

        (a) Functional baseline - system specifications (including key requirement tradeoffs, constraints, assumptions, and all data needed for certifications).

        (b) Allocated baseline - performance specifications (including key timing, design specs, and all data needed for certifications).

        (c) Product baseline - detailed specifications, processes, procedures, materiel, and technical documentation.

        (d) Source code/object code development and production including build documentation (e.g., data dictionary, thread maps, and message formats).

        (e) Peer review & other related quality process artifact control.

        (f) Prototype, model, and simulation version and documentation control.

        (g) Software/Systems Engineering Environment (S/SEE) tool configuration and documentation control (including operation and maintenance instruction, as applicable).

c. Provide requirements traceability and control to:

    (1) Show traceability of requirements from the original source, through all specifications and/or other documentation.

    (2) Include all derived interface and integration requirements.

    (3) Show traceability of requirements to design documentation and technical order source data.

d. Provide an integrated data management system with obsolescence precautions that:

    (1) Considers the use of non-developmental tools and interfaces with Government data management systems.

    (2) Considers Modular Open System Architecture (MOSA).

    (3) Allows single manager and developer immediate access.

    (4) Preserves trade study and other requirement decision rationale documentation.

e. Establish baselines of identified work products.

    (1) Identify the configuration items, components, and related work products, to include baseline documentation that will be placed under configuration control.

    (2) Identify the baseline versions of, and changes to, non-developmental and reused software.

    (3) Identify the interface and integration baseline.

    (4) Ensure developers maintain configuration control of all deliverable software and associated documentation at least until such time as the software development effort, including physical and functional configuration audits, is complete.

(5) Ensure developers maintain configuration control of the development environment including infrastructure.

(a) Ensure acquirers control the configuration of deliverable infrastructure and tools.

f. Create or release baselines for internal and operational use.

g. Establish and maintain the integrity of baselines:

(1) Establish and maintain technical data describing configuration items.

(2) Perform configuration audits to maintain integrity of the configuration baselines.

(3) Establish a configuration status accounting system to track baselines and product modifications throughout the life cycle.

3.12 Life Cycle Support

This section addresses several elements related to planning for and executing life cycle CS&S support. The real world of CS&S life cycle support offers challenges and opportunities, as the acquisition organization must maintain an eye to the future while balancing development program cost, schedule, and performance priorities. Throughout each budget execution year, the acquisition organization must manage the available resources, possibly reassessing the program priorities for that year. They may consider delaying out year requirements to continue current program execution, with the intention of obtaining additional resources to recover in the future. Such strategies can adversely impact the ability to effectively and efficiently sustain the system over the long term. This section will address strategies and planning to ensure delivered capabilities are sustainable throughout the lifecycle.

Aside from budget constraints, acquisition organizations are also pressured to meet development program schedule milestones. Because milestones are such obvious measures of a team's performance, there is immediate incentive to delay satisfaction of program requirements that may not be exposed until much later in the program. However, the delivered capabilities will not be sustainable unless sustainment has been properly planned and implemented.

Capability and performance requirements are readily measured and evaluated throughout acquisition, using Key Performance Parameters and Technical Performance Measures. Some aspects of suitability (e.g. reliability, maintainability, and transportability) also lend themselves to verification, but CS&S sustainability does not.

Another general consideration is the nature of software maintenance. Software repair involves returning a deficient design to specification or incorporating new requirements (originated or derived). The processes required to repair or maintain software are very similar to those used to develop it. Software repair requires requirement trades, design reiteration, interface control, prototyping, integration, testing, verification, fielding planning, and metrics.

During the development phases of acquisition, the stretch goal typically is to produce zero defect software. Realistically, the objective is to produce software that supports meeting system reliability, maintainability, and availability (RMA) requirements. Accomplishment of these goals/objectives is dependent on the successful balance of benefit, cost and schedule.

Once the software is in operational use, the increased exposure to operational use generates numerous requests for enhancements to improve suitability. An embedded system will also experience changes to its interfaces with externally controlled systems (e.g. weapons, joint operations enablers, sensor-to-kill chain). Resolution of all of these new requirements is usually deferred until the benefit justifies the cost.

3.12.1 Software Support Planning

It is important to plan during the development phase for the support of fielded computer systems and software. The planning process should begin early in the acquisition effort, and should be documented and coordinated with all relevant stakeholders. The planning should address the following activities:

    a. Support the determination of a support concept and source of post-deployment software support, based on analyses of the preliminary system's operational concept, other operational and support requirements, and Source of Repair Assignment Process (SORAP), as appropriate.

    b. As applicable, identify and agree on responsibilities of the acquisition, development, post-delivery support, test, and user organizations in planning and implementing the support capability.

c. Ensure all computer systems hardware, software, and engineering data that require support or are required to support the system are identified, and that the contractor is responsible for their development and delivery.

d. Establish a strategy to respond to hardware, software and support tools obsolescence (e.g., Diminishing Manufacturing Sources (DMS) issues).

e. Ensure training requirements are identified based on the selected life cycle support approach, including specific training requirements for the system's computer hardware and software components, and addressing the needs of both operational and support personnel.

f. Ensure the contractor identifies the human resources required to support the software, along with supporting rationale / assumptions.

g. Identify security requirements and ensure the contractor address their impact on system support.

h. Ensure the contractor defines the required computer resources support procedures, processes, and methods, and that they are coordinated with and acceptable to the support organizations and deliverable as part of the contract.

i. Establish criteria for transition of software sustainment responsibility from the contractor to the post deployment support organization, and include consideration of Government/contractor partnering opportunities for life cycle support.

j. If applicable, procure interim support to provide continuity of support subsequent to the completion of system development but prior to the availability of the permanent post-deployment software support organization.

k. In order to form a baseline for future integration, ensure the contractor documents initial software verification activities, including level of integration, fidelity of integration laboratories, and required flight test assets.

l. Procure (as required) and deliver all facilities, equipment, labs, tools and associated data required to support the software.

m. Ensure the contractor developed and deliverable labs and tools are documented sufficiently for support of transition to the supporting organization.

3.12.2 Software Product Engineering Data

Program offices should ensure that the minimum essential set of software product engineering data (documentation) is developed, acquired or escrowed, and maintained so that it is available to support sustainment needs for the full system life cycle. Software product engineering data includes specifications, architectural design, detailed design, interfaces, database design, software code, install and build scripts, tools and laboratories, test procedures and test cases, and related information such as change requests and problem reports. Software product engineering data also includes software development folders and the documented rationale that supported trade studies, exemptions, deviations, and waivers. Lack of quality product engineering data can lead to inefficiencies or re-work during sustainment, resulting in increased life-cycle costs. This problem can occur whether the product is maintained organically, through the original developer, or through an alternate support contractor.

Steps to ensure the availability of appropriate software product engineering data include:

a. Plan, program and budget the development and test of the S/SEEs and development and integration labs consistent with the needs of the system development program, and consider transferability of assets from development to sustainment at the outset.

b. Determining and contracting for the Software Product Engineering Data (SPED) of sufficient quality to support operation and sustainment needs throughout the system life-cycle.

c. Ensuring the contractor's process defines and captures the required SPED.

d. Ensuring the SPED is delivered and/or escrowed to enable effective and efficient long-term system support.

e. Establishing appropriate Government data rights consistent with the identified support concept.

3.12.3 Establish System/Software Engineering Environments and Associated Facilities

Adequate planning with regard to the software tools and facilities required by the contractor to design, develop, integrate, test, and support the CS&S is critical to the successful delivery and continued support of software driven capability. The following key steps should be considered:

a. In the RFP, solicit the offerors' approach to develop and support the S/SEE and development and integration labs with the needed capability and capacity.

b. Ensure the contractor identifies the complete set of S/SEE development and test tools necessary to accomplish the complete software effort, including PDSS. The contractor should apply the following planning / implementation process for the required development and test tools:

    (1) Ensure the contractor identifies the specific development and test tool requirements, the required level of tool integration, the need dates for each of the tools relative to the program schedule, the required performance/quality criteria for each tool, and an alternate management strategy if moderate to high risk is associated with the acquisition or development of the desired tool.

    (2) Ensure the contractor analyzes the program requirements and the development and test methodology, and establishes the appropriate software toolset for the development effort. Tools may be commercially acquired, selected from available in-house resources, or developed specifically for the program. However, the resources and lead-time associated with either purchasing or developing a new tool should be factored into the overall software development plan. Ensure adequate communication and coordination of the tool supplier schedules and the schedule of the development activity requiring the tool.

    (3) Ensure the contractor employs an open systems methodology to provide isolation of application software from the underlying hardware, in order to minimize adverse impact from the inevitable obsolescence and other diminishing manufacturing source issues.

    (4) Ensure the contractor baselines, controls, and demonstrates that newly acquired or developed (first-use) tools conform to established performance and quality criteria and that the staff is proficient in the use of these tools. Use of the tools for prototype development is encouraged as a means for demonstrating both software performance and staff proficiency.

    (5) Ensure that the developmental, runtime and enterprise licenses are obtained.

c. Ensure the contractor plans and budgets the acquisition or development and test of the S/SEEs and development and integration labs, consistent with the needs of the system development program.

d. Consider transferability of assets from development to production to sustainment, and budget accordingly.

e. Ensure the contractor analyzes requirements and plans/budgets for adequate spares for any flight-worthy or representative items Line Replaceable Units (LRUs) needed to support ground-based development and integration labs.

f. Ensure the contractor analyzes requirements and plans/budgets to satisfy security requirements for S/SEE and all associated ground based development and test environments. Ensure that the contract reflects appropriate security requirements.

g. If applicable, ensure the contractor plans and budgets to maintain a viable engineering team to support the CS&S products. Ensure that experience is retained and personnel turn-over is managed. Ensure the contractor provides for on-going training and certification. Anticipate the evolutionary nature of contractor-Government partnering.

3.12.4 Viable Life-Cycle Computer Systems and Software

It is an acquisition objective to develop and deliver computer systems and software that will provide capable, timely, and affordable functionality throughout all life cycle phases. This is accomplished by ensuring the contractor plans for the following:

a. The ability of the proposed computer system architecture to enable efficient and affordable design change/technology insertion (user capability requirements & technology refresh) over the life phases of the program (system development and demonstration, production and deployment, and operations and support).

b. The ability to efficiently and affordably produce and maintain a specification compliant system over the planned production schedule.

c. The ability to efficiently and affordably meet user requirements (e.g., availability, mission capable rate) for the economic life of the system as affected by product durability and technology obsolescence.

Some approaches that can be applied to support this objective include:

a. Selecting architectures which permit ease of change of underlying tools, languages, and hardware processing platforms.

b. Addressing hardware and software as an integrated system, not isolated entities.

c. Focusing on ease of changing the technology base, ease of verification, and ease of expansion to support future capability growth.

d. Exploring cross-cutting solutions to minimize proliferation of new architectures, components, and software.

For legacy systems:

a. Migrate over time toward more affordable and sustainable architectures and support environments.

b. Develop and implement a plan, including objectives, funding, and schedules, to accomplish this migration over the life cycle.

3.12.5 Computer Programming Language Selection

When a programming language decision must be made, programs should conduct a trade study to determine the best computer programming language, or mix of programming languages, to be used to satisfy system life cycle requirements. This includes the necessary criteria for PDSS. Suggested areas to be addressed include:

a. Language supports the planned application and architecture.

b. System / software requirements, including performance, interoperability, reliability, safety, security, architecture, partitioning, advanced functionality, and interface requirements.

c. Expected software size & complexity, system life-cycle change rate, and sustainment needs.

d. Reuse of existing systems / software (i.e., programming languages already being used within the system or within components from other sources that may be reused or adapted).

e. Language capabilities of the contractor.

f. Commercial viability of candidate languages, including current and future availability of compilers, tools, general-purpose development computer system equipment, training, and skilled software engineers.

g. Extent of compatibility with and impact of other related direction (e.g. use of standards such as the Joint Technical Architecture and open systems).

h. Languages defined by standards from organizations such as American National Standards Institute (ANSI) or International Standards Organization (ISO).

3.13 Lessons Learned

A lesson is not learned until it is put into practice or until behavior changes. In addition to this guidebook, there are many sources of lessons learned and opportunities for attaining needed awareness. The product center program management, engineering, financial management, and contracting organizations or the ACE office can provide assistance. Some additional resources follow:

a. *Defense Acquisition University (DAU)*

    (1) *Defense Acquisition Guidebook*

    (2) *Deskbook or Acquisition Knowledge Sharing System (AKSS)*

    (3) *Defense Acquisition University Training Center*

b. *Defense Technical Information Center (DTIC)*

    (1) *Scientific and Technical Information Network (STINET)*

c. Air Force Knowledge Now (AFKN) Communities of Practice (CoPs)

d. *Software Technology Support Center (STSC)* and *CrossTalk Journal*

e. Air Force Institute of Technology *Software Professional Development Program (SPDP)*

f. Space and Missile Systems Center (SMC) Software Acquisition Handbook

g. Aeronautical Systems Center (ASC) Software Acquisition Engineering Guidebook

h. Other service guidebooks and handbooks

i. Other Government agency guidebooks and handbooks

j. Industry conferences and seminars

k. Academia seminars and courses

Air Force Product Centers are expected to facilitate the collection of computer system and software related lessons learned and to share lessons learned between programs and with new programs. Program offices should contribute to a software lessons learned repository at their respective center by capturing and reporting the following at the conclusion of development for each block/increment:

a. Original estimates and delivered actuals for software size, effort, and schedule.

b. Program risks and mitigation approaches.

c. Objective descriptions of factors such as added or changed functional requirements, and schedule perturbations.

d. Other program events that contributed to successes and challenges, as noted above.

e. Processes that work well, processes that do not work well, processes that add no value, areas where new processes need to be developed, and processes that could not be addressed due to resource constraints.

f.   Reasons for any changes to required performance, increases in required resources, schedule extensions, changes in required or actual manpower, or any other factors or events that affect program outcome (cost, schedule, performance).

Appendix A
Software in the Integrated Master Plan

This section provides examples of software related content in the IMP, associated with various system level reviews. As noted elsewhere, the source selection team should perform an analysis of the specific software-related IMP content.

Software development activities for development approaches other than the Waterfall Development process include all activities of the Waterfall. For example, the preliminary design for each increment or block should be followed by an incremental PDR. The detail design for each increment should be followed by an incremental CDR. In all development approaches the program office should include a mini-audit following each incremental review to assure all items have been completed. Incremental reviews can also be used in a Waterfall Development. The incremental event enables smaller portions of the project to be reviewed and enables greater insight by the project office.

It should be noted that the use of new software development approaches, such as Agile Methods, does not relieve the developer of the requirement to conduct deliberate and thoughtful reviews to ensure the product is evolving to meet cost, schedule, and performance objectives.

It should also be noted that these requirements apply not only to the prime contractor, but also to subcontractors where they have significant software development responsibility.

TABLE A- 1 presents a sample listing of IMP software-related entry and exit criteria for system level reviews.

TABLE A- 1. Entry and Exit Criteria Sample.

IMP Event	Criteria
Alternative Systems Review (ASR): Preferred alternative system concepts established	**Entry Criteria:** • Applicable trade studies or other analyses have been conducted and a preferred solution identified. • All required documents are established and delivered **Exit Criteria:** • Computer System & Software (CS&S) architectural trade off analyses identified, including architectural alternatives • Hardware vis-à-vis software functional trade-off analyses identified • Software demonstration and prototyping requirements identified • Key software technologies defined • CS&S risks identified with effective risk management strategy defined • Concept and Technology Development (C&TD) software development requirements defined • C&TD software development processes defined (contractors' plans) • Test and Evaluation Master Plan (TEMP) updated to reflect analyses and trade-off findings • All action items are dispositioned and where appropriate, closed

System Requirements Review (SRR: System requirements established)	**Entry Criteria:** • C&TD software development requirements defined • C&TD software development processes defined (contractors plan) • All required documents are established and delivered **Exit Criteria:** • CS&S high level requirements defined in the System Specification • CS&S demonstrations and prototyping plans are defined • Preliminary software development process defined and documented • Initial software development size estimates defined • Software trade-offs addressing COTS, reuse, development risks, and architectures are identified and planned • Initial allocation of functional requirements to hardware, software, and personnel defined • Initial System/Software Engineering Environment (S/SEE) integrated software development tool requirements defined • Software development training requirements identified • Preliminary SD&D phase software development estimates established with effort, schedule, and cost analysis • Programming languages and architectures, security requirements and operational and support concepts have been identified • Preliminary software support data defined • TEMP updated to reflect the requirements allocation and trade-offs • All action items are dispositioned and where appropriate, closed
System Functional Review (SFR): Functional and performance requirements established	**Entry Criteria:** • All required documents are established and delivered **Exit Criteria:** • CS&S requirements in the System Specification are complete • Draft Preliminary Software Requirements Specifications defined, including complete verification requirements • Initial CS&S architecture design is defined • System/segment design approach defined, including the software architecture • Software development process defined and reflected in IMP • Specification tree is defined through subsystem development specifications, including interface specifications • Draft subsystem/allocated functional specifications, including CS&S requirements, are complete • Preliminary identification of the System/Software Engineering Environment tools and configuration is defined • CS&S design/development approach confirmed through analyses, demonstrations, and prototyping • Software process IMP/IMS events, schedule, task definitions, and metrics updated to reflect subsystem/allocated functional specification and further defined for the next phase • Software requirements traceability defined through the higher tier specifications to the system/subsystem requirements • Preliminary software risk management process refined • Contract work breakdown structure defines all necessary software development work, consistent with the defined software development processes for the SD&D phase • All necessary software development work consistent with the contractors defined software development process for the SD&D phase is defined in the CWBS

	• Software development estimates for SD&D phase completed • Software Development Plan (SDP) completed • TEMP updated to incorporate subsystem and integration test requirements • All action items are dispositioned and where appropriate, closed
Software Specification Review (SSR): software requirements established [internal contractor baseline]	**Entry Criteria:** • Complete Software Requirements Specification (SRS) for each CSCI • Complete Interface Requirements Specifications (IRSs) • All required documents are established and delivered **Exit Criteria:** • Software development risk management process defined • Software and interface requirements established in internal baselines • Requirements allocation for first increment or for all planned increments (blocks/builds) defined (as applicable) • Software and interface requirements allocated to CSCIs and Computer Software Units (CSU's) • Software requirements traceability between system/subsystem specifications and software requirements specification refined • Software development schedules reflecting contractor selected processes and IMP/IMS events for CSCIs and CSUs refined • Software metrics defined • Prototypes and demonstrations identified and planned • Life-cycle software support requirements defined • Software requirements verification matrix established • Software development test facilities defined • Software size control program defined • Software development estimates updated • CS&S architecture requirements defined • S/SEE tools and configuration requirements defined • TEMP refined to reflect the CSCI and CSU test facilities and plans • All action items are dispositioned and where appropriate, closed
Preliminary Design Review (PDR): software architectural design established [internal contractor baseline]	**Entry Criteria:** • SRS and IRS are internally (developmental) baselined • Software development process definition baselined and linked to IMP/IMS • Software Specification Review (SSR) has been successfully completed • Preliminary software design is defined and documented • All required documents are established and delivered **Exit Criteria:** • Software risk management process refined and implemented • Software architectural level design established • S/SEE requirements and configuration are defined and internally controlled • Software requirements baseline verified to satisfy system/subsystem functional requirements baseline • Software increments (blocks and builds) defined and allocated • Preliminary ICDs defined and documented • Software metrics refined and implemented • Software test plan refined and documented • Initial plans established for software tools and software test environment validation • Initial analysis to demonstrate requirements closure complete

	• Initial evaluation of reused/COTS/OSS software completed • Life-cycle software support requirements updated • Software development process defined and implemented • Software development estimates updated • TEMP updated as needed to reflect any software increment testing • All action items are dispositioned and where appropriate, closed
Critical Design Review (CDR): detailed software design established [internal contractor baseline]	**Entry Criteria:** • Software detailed design is complete • All required documents are established and delivered **Exit Criteria:** • Software requirements traceability established • Software detailed level design established • ICDs complete • Software test descriptions complete • Draft software test procedures complete • Detailed software design and interface descriptions complete • Software metrics defined and implemented • Software development files established and maintained current • Analysis to demonstrate design addresses all software requirements is complete • Evaluation of reused/COTS/OSS software updated • Software development estimates updated • Software tools and software test environment validation completed • TEMP updated to reflect test plans • All action items are dispositioned and where appropriate, closed
Test Readiness Review (TRR): test readiness established [internal contractor baseline]	**Entry Criteria:** • Software design and code is internally baselined • Software requirements, design, and code traceability is established • Software test plan complete • Software test descriptions and procedures are defined, verified, baselined, and compliant with plan • Software test procedures are adequate to verify specified requirements • Software tools and software test environment validated • Test facilities and resources are complete and sufficient to support software testing within the defined schedule • All required documents are established and delivered **Exit Criteria:** • Planned testing is consistent with defined incremental approach including regression testing • Software unit and computer software component (CSC) testing is complete and documented in the software development files (SDFs) • Test facilities/resources/measurement techniques verified to support verification • Software metrics show readiness for testing • Software problem report system is defined and implemented • Software test baseline is established • Software development estimates are updated • All action items are dispositioned and where appropriate, closed

Functional Configuration Audit (FCA): system / software performance and functional requirements verified	**Entry Criteria:** • CSCIs are verified through all levels of hardware / software integration and test, and through subsystem integration and test • Software product specification is complete • CSCI test results are documented and CSCIs are acceptable for intended use • All required documents are established and delivered **Exit Criteria:** • Software product specifications are baselined (including source code listings) • Software requirements, design, and code traceability are established • Software test reports are approved • Software development files are complete • CS&S functional and performance requirements have been verified against the specified system requirements through analysis of test results • Required operational and support manuals / documents are complete • All action items are dispositioned and where appropriate, closed • All required software completion criteria are satisfied
Physical Configuration Audit (PCA): product baseline established	**Entry Criteria:** • All software documentation is complete and available for audit **Exit Criteria:** • Software product specification is verified against the as-built product • Software support and operational data is complete and verified for accuracy • Version description documents are completed and verified for accuracy • Software metrics are complete • All action items are dispositioned and where appropriate, closed

Appendix B
Software Content for the
Statement of Objectives (SOO)
and Statement of Work (SOW)

This section provides example language related to the acquisition of software intensive systems that can be applied to the SOO or SOW, as appropriate. Not all example objectives or tasks are applicable to all programs.

B.1   Example SOO Objectives

a. An efficient development program that balances risk, cost, schedule and performance.

b. Phased development via incremental software/hardware development approaches.

c. A comprehensive systems engineering process to specify, design, develop, integrate, test, produce, deliver, verify, validate, document, and sustain the system/software that:

   (1) Satisfies all System Requirements Document (SRD)/Technical Requirements Document (TRD)/ Capabilities Development Document (CDD) threshold requirements.

   (2) Supports rapid, cost effective development/modification of the operational system, training system, and support components to meet SRD thresholds and as many objectives as are affordable.

   (3) Includes the ability to easily and inexpensively upgrade existing equipment and/or insert new technologies as they become available.

   (4) Mitigates the risks associated with technology obsolescence, proprietary technologies, and reliance on a single source of supply over the life of the system.

   (5) Ensures interoperability with the Global Information Grid (GIG) systems and ground processing infrastructures.

   (6) Reduces system life cycle cost and logistics footprint by addressing required quality attributes, such as reliability, maintainability, supportability, safety, security, and human factors.

   (7) Supports rapid, cost effective modification/upgrade/technology insertion.

d. An effective system/software development and integration process that uses a modular open systems architecture approach.

e. Timely deployment of initial training components.

f. Use of contractor management processes, procedures, systems, internal metrics, and performance measures unless their use conflicts with contract requirements or does not allow contract requirements to be completely met.

g. Timely, cost effective transition to organic support that ensures access to all required technical data and computer software, and associated license rights.

h. Development/production/delivery of a Technical Data Package (TDP) that ensures the Government's ability to support the system over the life cycle.

B.2   Example SOW Tasks

a. The contractor shall establish the CS&S architecture within the context of the overall system including selection of processor types and architecture, and software architecture and major interfaces, in accordance with applicable Open Systems guidance. As applicable, the SOW should describe which architecture evaluation steps are the supplier's responsibilities, and which are to be performed jointly by the acquirer and the system supplier.

b. The contractor shall generate a specification, SOW, WBS in accordance with the CDRL, IMP, IMS, and SDP sufficient to describe the software development processes to be employed on the program.

c. The contractor shall design, fabricate, integrate, test, and evaluate the hardware, software, facilities, personnel subsystems, training, and the principle items necessary to satisfy program requirements, and to support and operate the system. This includes the requirements analysis, design, coding and unit testing, component integration and testing, and CSCI level testing for software. This also includes system development and operational test and evaluation, software quality, configuration management, and support for software.

d. The contractor shall define a software development approach appropriate for the computer software development and integration effort to be performed under this solicitation.

e. The contractor shall document the software development approach in a SDP, shall implement the SDP requirements, and shall maintain the SDP.

   (1) The SDP shall describe the contractor's software development and quality processes. These processes should be based on the contractor's tailoring of internally-developed standard processes used on previous military programs, standard commercial processes, and wholly new standard processes. Software processes documented in the SDP shall be integrated and consistent with the IMP and IMS.

   (2) The contractor shall comply with the requirements of the SDP for all computer software to be developed, integrated, or maintained under this effort. The SDP shall identify the required software and the developers or suppliers of the software, and shall define the offeror's proposed software development processes, the activities to be performed as a part of the processes, the tasks which support the activities, and the techniques and tools to be used to perform the tasks.

   Note: The Government at its discretion may place the SDP on contract. Refer to Appendix I for suggested SDP content.

f. The contractor shall support the CS&S IPT as appropriate. This group shall be responsible to:

   (1) Define the computer systems and software architecture.

   (2) Plan the development and delivery of all software components, blocks.

(3) Monitor the progress and status of all CS&S activities.

(4) Manage CS&S risks.

(5) Advise the program manager in all areas relating to the acquisition and support of computer resources.

(6) Select and document a software support concept.

(7) Monitor compliance of the program with computer systems and software policy, plans, procedures, and standards.

(8) Integrate software test activities with the overall system test plan/approach.

g. The contractor shall use EVM to manage, determine the status of, and report on the software development effort.

h. The contractor shall implement selected software metrics to provide management visibility into the software development process and progress. The contractor shall apply the Air Force core software metrics, as a minimum. The selected metrics shall clearly portray variances between actual and planned performance, shall provide early detection or prediction of situations that require management attention, and shall support the assessment of the impact of proposed changes on the program. The contractor shall provide the program office routine insight into these metrics. Note: Refer to Appendix H of this guidebook for more information on the Air Force Core Software Metrics.

i. The contractor shall define, manage, track, and verify computer resources (hardware/software) growth and reserve capacity requirements as defined in the system and subsystem specifications. This includes reserve capacity for memory, throughput, I/O, and network.

j. The contractor shall perform a growth analysis for each functional area considering historical experience and risk, software size control activities, planned technology refresh upgrades to computer resources hardware based on predictions, and qualification of hardware necessary to support growth provisions.

k. The contractor shall include software processes, tasks, reviews, and events in the IMP and IMS. The contractor shall ensure the SDP, IMP, and IMS include the processes, events, and criteria to manage the technical performance characteristics and associated margins and tolerances of the hardware and software.

l. The contractor shall address computer systems and software as part of technical reviews and audits. [Refer to Appendix B for more information on software coverage in technical reviews and audits.]

m. The contractor shall perform special studies as requested by the Government (e.g. design trade studies, cost benefit analyses, and CS&S maintenance/upgrade plans).

n. The Government intends to establish and achieve full organic maintenance capability for the system and separately contract for Training Systems (Aircrew Training System/ Maintenance Training System (ATS/MTS)) development & procurement. Successful establishment and achievement of this capability requires the contractor and subcontractors to compile, control, maintain and deliver various engineering design disclosure data including computer software in varying media forms and methods in accordance with {specific Contract Line Item Number (CLINs) and contract clauses}.

o.   The contractor shall implement procedures to ensure early identification of all asserted restrictions on all technical data and computer software (both commercial and noncommercial), including restrictions asserted by subcontractors and suppliers, and to manage the use of proprietary technologies.

p.   The contractor shall prepare and provide Software Resources Data Reports (SRDRs). SRDR requirements, in accordance with DoD 5000.04-M-1, shall apply to the prime and be flowed down to any lower tier contractor that will have an SD&D contract for software effort valued at more than $25M.

q.   The contractor shall establish and maintain a hardware-in-the-loop, software/system integration lab (SIL). [Note: may not be applicable/required for all weapon system programs.]

r.   The contractor shall implement a program to provide quality assurance of software processes and deliverables. Develop and maintain a Software Quality Assurance Plan which details the subsystem and system level processes used to insure software products are tested and validated in accordance with the systems engineering requirements decomposition. Major events within the Software Quality Assurance Plan shall be reflected in the IMS. Major events include, but are not limited to, Software Quality Audits, Software Configuration Audits, and Software Qualification Testing. Software Quality Assurance shall be flowed to vendors and subcontractors that produce software products used in meeting program requirements.

s.   The contractor shall develop, implement, and maintain a Software Requirements Specification (SRS), a Software Design Description (SDD), a System/Subsystem Design Description (SSDD), and a Software Product Specification (SPS).

t.   The contractor shall maintain the approved System Specification. The Government will control the functional baseline as reflected in the System Specification and the contractor shall control the allocated and product baseline (software and hardware) throughout the development phase.

u.   The contractor shall establish and maintain a configuration and data management process (hardware and software) for the duration of the program, using MIL-HDBK-61A as a guide. The contractor shall develop, implement, and maintain a Configuration Management/Data Management Plan that addresses the entire life cycle. The contractor shall establish and maintain an electronic data management system that facilitates Government access.

v.   The contractor shall provide appropriate technical data and license rights for the entire system. For any unmodified commercial off the shelf (COTS) systems, this includes at least the deliverables and license rights as are typically provided to the customer or end user, and at least the minimum rights for technical data as required by DFARS 252.227-7015. For all other systems (e.g., noncommercial, military peculiar, or developmental - including any modifications to commercial systems that are funded in whole or in part by the Government), this includes (1) the complete technical data package providing all production-level details; (2) all computer software as defined at DFARS 252.227-7014, including object/executable code, source code, and design information; and (3) the associated license rights consistent with the applicable Defense Federal Acquisition Regulation Supplement (DFARS) data rights clauses (including/allowing specially negotiated license rights when appropriate). [Note: contractors should be required to provide *early* notification of any software they deem proprietary and should provide supporting rationale.]

w. The contractor shall develop, implement and maintain a System Safety Program (SSP), in accordance with MIL-STD-882D. The SSP shall assess hardware, software safety, human factors, and other potential sources of hazards for acceptable mishap risk throughout the system life cycle, such as safety critical functions. The contractor shall document the SSP in a SSPP per data item DI-SAFT-81626, 1 August 2001. The SSPP shall describe the contractor's proposed system safety program in detail, including processes to identify typical hazards and develop design solutions for them, and identify candidate hazards for analysis. Assessments shall be accomplished using best commercial/military system safety practices to analyze system design, software, and pilot-vehicle interface issues. The contractor shall propose a methodology for verification testing of safety critical items.

Appendix C
Example Software Content for RFP Section L

RFP Section L defines expected content for offeror proposals. Specifically, Section L is used to ensure that the information necessary to evaluate Section M factors and subfactors is requested, and that information that will not be evaluated is not requested.

The list of example Section L items provided here, while not exhaustive, addresses typical areas of concern related to software. Items must be thoughtfully selected, tailored, matched to Section M evaluation factors and subfactors, and integrated into an RFP, focusing on those that will be discriminators for the solicitation.

While the case cannot be made that each of these example items are discriminators individually, collectively they form the basis for demonstrating that effective processes are established. Such processes have proven to be a critical element in the successful development of large, complex software systems.

RFP Sections L and M must be consistent. Example content is provided here simply for consideration in developing RFPs for specific programs and is not provided in a manner that tracks directly to the example content for RFP Section M provided in Appendix D.

Offerors should be encouraged to demonstrate commitment to the proposed software development approach and processes by incorporating into the proposed SOW those specific tasks necessary to define, develop, test, and deploy the CS&S within the context of the overall system development. The CS&S tasks in the SOW should be consistent with the development processes proposed in the SDP, IMP, IMS, and verification sections of the specifications. Offerors should also be encouraged to reference the proposed Software Development Plan (SDP) when responding to RFP requirements.

The following example content is provided for RFP Section L:

   a. Define a software development approach appropriate for the CS&S development effort to be performed under this solicitation. Document this approach in a proposed SDP that describes the software engineering development, quality, and integrity processes, activities, and tasks the offeror is committing to employ on the program, identifying specific standards, methods, tools, actions, strategies, and responsibilities. The SDP shall be coordinated and consistent with the IMP, IMS, SOO, SOW and section 4 (verification) of the proposed specifications. Proposed processes should be based on the tailoring of standard developer processes. The SDP shall address all software including both deliverable and non-deliverable products developed. For new processes not yet documented, describe the benefits and risks and the rationale for employing them. Provide examples of any "just-in-time" procedures and checklists, explain how such checklists are developed (such as tailoring from existing company standard process templates), and, if applicable, describe any tailoring guidance. [Note: Content from Appendix I, Software Development Plan, may be included in the RFP to drive offeror SDP content.]

   b. Describe the proposed software life cycle model (Waterfall, incremental). Identify any proposed incremental development and verification processes and the use of system analysis and trades, modeling and simulation, prototyping to mitigate technical and schedule risk. Identify proposed capability blocks/increments.

c. Describe the process for establishing the CS&S architecture within the context of the overall system. Describe the process for selecting system architecture, processor types, software architecture, and major interfaces. Describe how the process considers incorporation of open architecture/technology in the system design process. Describe how the architecture development process considers functional/performance requirements, safety and security, reserve computing and communications capacity, ease of growth/expansion, and technology refresh. Identify new hardware components as well as those that are modified or already exist and are used as-is. Identify specific planned hardware modifications. Also describe how the process considers software layering, real-time operating system considerations, structural hierarchy, CSCIs, CSCs, and CSUs. Identify the hardware configurations coupled to the software versions.

d. Identify all proposed CS&S components to the extent they are defined and known in the proposal timeframe. Describe the process for identifying CSCIs. Define the parameters used in the selection process (e.g. size, target processor, performance, and cost). Describe how this process integrates with the system engineering requirements definition and allocation process.

e. Describe how CS&S risks are identified and tracked in the program/system level risk management system. Describe how risk management is applied to software subcontractors and suppliers. Identify the initial set of CS&S related risks, and describe how resources are identified to deal with them.

f. Provide sizing information for the expected CS&S hardware and software. The CSCI/CSC functions identified should be based on the offeror's preliminary allocation of functions to hardware and software. Provide separate size, effort (hours), schedule, and staffing estimates for each CSCI/CSC function identified. Provide discussion, justification and validation for the functions and estimates. List all estimating assumptions, including those for growth in software size during system development. Describe any measures proposed to control software size growth. Address separately any subcontracted software development efforts.

g. For any proposed software reuse/COTS components, provide the following information (to the extent possible):

(1) Describe the process for selecting the software.

(2) Describe the development organization's familiarity with the proposed software, and explain the extent to which the proposed software is operational in a similar mission application and architecture.

(3) Identify the software (by version) planned for use for this application.

(4) Identify the source of the proposed software, by program or project.

(5) Identify the size and programming language for the proposed software.

(6) Provide a detailed functional description of the proposed software.

(7) Describe the level of insight into and analysis of the detailed software requirements and design.

(8) Justify with analyses and criteria why the proposed software is a credible candidate for this application.

(9) Describe differences in performance and interface requirements between the proposed software as it exists and its application on this program.

(10) Identify the existing functionality planned for use on this application.

(11) Identify the existing functionality not required for this application.

(12) Describe the current maturity of the proposed software (i.e. requirements complete, preliminary design complete, detailed design complete, coding complete, software fully qualified, system integration testing in SIL complete, currently flying/operational, configuration audits complete, known deficiencies).

(13) Describe the expected maturity of the proposed software at the time it will be imported.

(14) Identify and justify any required changes, including specific areas of change and amount of redesign, new/modified lines of code, and retest/re-verification.

(15) Characterize the complexity of any required changes to the proposed software.

(16) Quantify the technical risks associated with modifying the software for us in this application.

(17) Identify how the proposed software will be functionally integrated into this application, and describe the integration complexity.

(18) Explain in detail how the software/system will be formally qualified (and certified, if applicable).

(19) Describe the plan for post-deployment support of the proposed software, and address intellectual property rights and licensing. Describe the approach for keeping the software in a supportable configuration over the program life cycle. Discuss access to source code.

(20) For reuse software, describe the confidence in achieving the proposed level of reuse and at the same time avoiding overall software growth and program impact while satisfying all program requirements. Justify any proposed trade-offs in performance to allow higher levels of reuse with attendant program benefits.

(21) Identify the activities, effort, cost, and schedule required to integrate the proposed software.

(22) Describe the volatility/stability of the proposed software, and describe how the program will deal with associated changes and updates. Identify who controls the future evolution of the software.

h. Identify any proposed use of NDI such as Government furnished equipment (GFE), property (GFP), software (GFS), or information (GFI), or OSS. Describe any assumptions regarding the content, completeness, and quality of proposed NDI. Identify any risks associated with the use of NDI software and describe risk mitigation plans. Specifically define the process for integrating NDI with newly developed hardware and software. Describe the approach to assure that the selected NDI will meet the performance and functional requirements in the system specification. Describe the interaction with the NDI developer, including how content and baselines are controlled, how many baselines are supported, and how product/system performance will be evaluated as the NDI baseline changes over time.

i. Describe the software requirements process. Describe the overarching system and subsystem requirements design process that must be completed prior to the completion of software level requirements. Explain how the process provides traceability between the SRS and higher level requirements. Explain how the process ties specification section 4 verification requirements to section 3 performance requirements. If an incremental/block development approach is proposed, define the increment/block content and explain how the requirements process identifies the target increment/block where each performance requirement will be implemented and verified.

j.   As part of the proposed SDP, describe how the software development will be managed. Identify the software metrics proposed for use on this development effort, including any metrics that are in addition to the Air Force core metrics. Describe how the metrics will be used to manage the software development effort, and how they will be adapted as the needs of the program change. Describe how metrics data will be rolled-up and presented to provide a consistent picture that spans the development team. Describe how metrics information will be communicated to the Government. [Note: Software metrics are described in guidebook section 3.7, and Air Force core metrics are described in Appendix H.]

k.   Discuss the methodology for defining, managing, tracking and verifying computer resources (hardware/software) growth and reserve capacity requirements. Include the approach to growth analysis for each functional area considering historical experience and risk, planned or predicted technology refresh or other upgrades to computer resources hardware, qualification of hardware necessary to support growth provisions. Describe the process to assure a complete definition of software requirements, including dependencies relative to timing and throughput.

l.   Describe how the planned CS&S work is defined within the EVM system. Describe how this definition correlates with the Contract Work Breakdown Structure (CWBS), SOW, IMP and IMS. Describe the process for establishing software EVM tracking and reporting. Define the guidelines for establishing software development work packages at the lowest level (e.g., maximum hours, number of people, maximum duration, and duration between measurement milestones). Specifically address the process for establishing work packages whose size is consistent with timely identification of problems concerning actual expenditures versus earned value. Describe the criteria for taking earned value on individual tasks, e.g., 0 - 100%, 50 - 50%, supervisor's estimate, percent complete. Describe how EVM data will be rolled-up and presented to provide a consistent picture that spans the development team.

m.   Identify any proposed software or documentation with limited or restricted rights, provide rationale, and identify any licensing agreements that apply to the S/SEE that may affect the Government's ability to operate or support the software organically or by a third party.

n.   Discuss how the proposed approach ensures a robust system design (fault tolerant, allowance for manufacturing variability). Explain the approach to software development in the context of concurrent hardware/software development with critical timing, through-put, and memory constraints.

o.   Describe the process to identify safety critical software and to ensure it will function safely relative to the CS&S implementation. Address the following:

    (1)   <u>Hazard Analyses</u>: Describe the techniques used to determine the safety critical functions and software components of these functions. Describe how this will be accomplished at the system and subsystem level for both requirements and design.

    (2)   <u>Software Development Process</u>: Identify and describe specific software development process methods, steps, and tools which will be applied to safety

critical software components. Address requirements through the design and implementation phases.

    (3) <u>Testing</u>: Describe the verification methods utilized to ensure the integrity of safety critical function and their associated software. Describe how hazards associated with safety critical functions will be eliminated or controlled to an acceptable level of risk. Identify the role each of the following levels of testing plays in this verification process: system testing, subsystem testing, hardware/software integration testing, and all levels of software development testing. Link lower level testing to overall Developmental Test and Evaluation (DT&E) and Operational Test and Evaluation (OT&E) planning and execution, including completion of the Verification Cross Reference Matrix. Describe how FMET is applied to safety critical hardware and software. Describe how the proposed system and software architecture mitigates risk associated with failures. Describe the fault tolerance of the system for single failures, dual failures, and combination failures and the consequential results of the failure(s). Describe the overall software testing and regression testing approach, including requirements for various levels of test (e.g., CSU, CSC, CSC Integration, CSCI, systems integration testing) to ensure that all safety critical software is fully qualified for each flight release.

p. Describe in the proposed SDP, the process to define the mission critical software protection requirements, including:

    (1) Analyses to define system threats to and vulnerabilities of the weapon system development environment.

    (2) Analyses to define the requirements and the modes of operation of the development and support environment to protect against malicious infiltration of the environment.

    (3) Analyses to define the requirements for protection against computer viruses (capable of self propagation through the system), sabotage, and insertion of hidden damage vehicles (e.g., deliberate errors) capable of disrupting either the development and support environment operation or the safety and operational effectiveness of the produced weapon system.

    (4) Physical security, administrative controls, development system connectivity and the use of software systems and process designed to aid in maintaining system security and integrity.

    (5) Protection requirements derived from operational requirements (as defined in the system specification) which impact the development environment, the weapon system design/architecture or its operation.

    (6) Other factors, as defined by the offeror determined to be critical to the protection of the environment and the operational weapon system.

q. Describe how the architecture will process both classified and unclassified data simultaneously and meet IA requirements identified in <u>DoDD 8500.1</u>. Describe the integration of the IA process into the systems engineering process, including cost benefit trades. Address security vulnerabilities in COTS/reuse components.

r. Describe the corrective action system for problem reporting, categorization/prioritization, tracking, resolution, and review boards.

s.   Describe the software quality assurance tasks, including the means and timing by which the software processes and products will be analyzed and evaluated. In this context, the analyses and evaluations include vendors and subcontractors and shall examine: 1) the requirements allocation to software, 2) the adherence to design disciplines, 3) the adherence to coding disciplines, 4) the lower level testing and anomaly resolution, 5) the adherence to integration disciplines, 6) the subsystem and system level testing and anomaly resolution, 7) the qualification and validation of software, 8) the criteria used in software quality audits, 9) the criteria used in configuration audits, 10) the criteria used to assure software is free from any type of malicious code, 11) the software configuration control through delivery of software products, and 12) the corrective action system.

t.   Describe the CS&S support management process. Specifically address the support management process role in design and development, test and evaluation planning, and other key program phases and events. Describe how the following elements of the computer resources support management process ensure support requirements will be satisfied:

(1)   Integration of CS&S support with the systems engineering process.

(2)   CS&S support integration into design trade studies.

(3)   Facilities and capital requirements for CS&S support.

(4)   CS&S support integration with the integrated logistics support process.

(5)   CS&S support integration with the software IPT/computer resources working group.

(6)   Experience gained in using this process on other commercial or Government programs, the results obtained, and any associated metrics.

u.   Describe the documents, reviews, and corresponding entrance/exit criteria for the software requirements definition, design, coding, test, and integration phases.

v.   Describe the process for selecting the programming implementation language for each CSCI. Describe the risk management activities planned to achieve the required programming language capabilities consistent with the program's need dates. Describe how the selected programming language tools are integrated into the S/SEE. Describe the specific characteristics and parameters to be considered in the programming language selection process.

w.   Define and incorporate into the proposed IMP the specific software tasks, reviews, events consistent with the proposed development processes, clearly indicating the sequencing of development tasks and milestones, and allocating adequate time and resources to apply the proposed processes. Define clear software product completion criteria and methods of incremental verification to establish software product completion. Ensure these criteria are consistent with section 4 of the proposed specifications. Incorporate critical events for increments/blocks of routine and safety critical software development into appropriate sections of the IMP. [Note: See Appendix A, "Software in the Integrated Master Plan." The Government at its discretion may place the proposed IMP on contract.]

x.   Define and incorporate into the proposed IMS the specific software tasks consistent with the proposed development processes. Define task durations and resource loading for each IMS software event.

y.   Describe the approach to supporting Government validation of system capabilities, including analysis of algorithms, analysis tools, and system performance simulation and validation tools.

z.   Describe the process for providing the Government with access to both developmental and product baseline data generated on the S/SEE. Describe the approach to availability and utilization of the S/SEE across the contractor (prime/sub/associate) and Government team members (applicable acquisition, logistics, and test centers). Identify S/SEE assets that will be required for sustainment, including those which are contractor-furnished.

aa. Describe the software product engineering data (documentation) that will be developed and maintained as part of the software development/sustainment effort. Provide rationale.

bb. Describe the configuration and data management process for the program.

cc. Provide the software cost data and assumptions used for all planned deliverable and non-deliverable software developed or used on this contract and previous contract efforts. Provide the definitions used for software cost estimating for this contract and previous related contract efforts.

dd. The offeror shall build a software parametric file using the *<insert applicable model>* software parametric estimating model. The offeror shall model the software parametric file based on the software development concept and provide the model and completed Parametric Data Sheets on a CD-ROM disk for Government evaluation. The electronic software development file shall be built at a CSCI level, and shall include subcontracted software, COTS, GOTS, reuse from a legacy program, and/or new development items. For COTS items, potential suppliers and costs shall be included in the Basis of Estimate (RFP Section L attachment *<insert applicable attachment number>*). Potential suppliers and costs shall be included in the offeror's generated software model. For GOTS software, the offeror shall provide information on the supplying Government agency to include points of contact, so the Government can verify the size and CSCI/CSC maturity level. Any GOTS software should be included in the offeror's PRICE S model for integration purposes. If the CSCI/CSC relies on legacy code (currently existing), the offeror shall provide the program name, size, and description of program maturity (e.g. legacy software developed under company Independent Research & Development (IR&D) legacy software development on XYZ aircraft program). The offeror shall provide a CWBS number reference within the CSCI/CSC description. The offeror shall address software growth within the software parametric model. The offeror shall make use of the "Notes" capability within the software estimating model to clearly define how inputs were derived or to document any ground rules or assumptions made. Such parametric inputs and resulting model shall be clearly reconcilable with the offeror's proposal. The offeror shall use the SLOC definition below to build their model:

> Source Lines of Code (SLOC) is a size unit parameter that represents the number of logical lines of code of the software component. This value is usually determined by counting the number of delimiters (e.g. semi-colons). Comments are excluded from the SLOC count. This definition means that a SLOC (1) may extend over more than one physical line, (2) represents a complete statement in the implementation language, and (3) includes executable and nonexecutable statements, but not comments.

ee. The offeror shall adjust the software estimating model to match the proposed software development process and business structure by adjusting the global, escalation, and financial factor's tables within the model. Additionally, the offeror shall address, within the basis of estimate (BOE), how software growth is included.

ff. The offeror shall identify each software activity in the IMS. Each CSCI (developed, modified or purchased requiring development or modification) required to implement the offeror's technical solution shall be represented as a separate activity in the IMS. The duration of the CSCI activities shall be based on the total time required to accomplish all phases of development/modification for that CSCI (e.g. requirements analysis, preliminary/detail design, code and unit test and CSC integration and test) and shall correspond to the dates submitted on parametric input sheets. Unmodified legacy CSCIs shall not be represented in the IMS. Additionally, the IMS shall contain a milestone titled "SW Complete," which indicates the completion of all SW development, modification, integration and verification activities.

gg. Offeror shall describe the approach to develop and manage CSDRs.

Appendix D
Example Software Content for RFP Section M

The AFMC Contracting Solicitation Section M Guide and Template provides the following guidance:

"When reviewing the SOO, Performance Specification, and CDRL, the program office team should decide what's important or risky (from requirements and risk analysis); determine the evaluation factors and subfactors required to discriminate between offerors regarding the important or risky parts of the program or effort, and then formulate Section M subfactors for them. Each subfactor under the Mission Capability factor should include the minimum performance or capability requirements the offeror must meet to be deemed acceptable, and both threshold and objective values where appropriate. The subfactor should be worded so that an offeror's mere inclusion of a topic in its proposal will not result in a determination that the proposal is acceptable with regard to that subfactor. Instead, the subfactor should be written to expect a proposal discussion that offers a sound approach and which describes a system/design which will meet the solicitation's requirements and can be achieved within the schedule (specified in the solicitation or proposed in the offer)."

The guide and template also states that Sections L and M must track to one another. Once the evaluation factors and subfactors have been developed, "Section L is then written to include proposal instructions, ensuring that the information necessary to evaluate the factors and subfactors is requested and information that will not be evaluated is not requested."

The following subfactor and associated measures of merit are provided as examples. The measures of merit may be duplicative in some areas, and must be tailored for use in a specific solicitation. Note also that Air Force Federal Acquisition Regulation Supplement (AFFARS) Mandatory Procedure 5315.3 (Source Selection) requires that "Systems Engineering shall be a mission capability subfactor in all ACAT program acquisitions, and in all other acquisitions where systems engineering effort is required." Some of the measures of merit provided as examples below for software may duplicate some of what would be expected in the Systems Engineering subfactor, and again must be tailored for use in a specific solicitation. While the case cannot be made that each of these example factors/subfactors are discriminators individually, collectively they form the basis for demonstrating that effective processes are established. Such processes have proven to be a critical element in the successful development of large, complex software systems.

RFP Sections L and M must be consistent. Example content is provided here simply for consideration in developing RFPs for specific programs and is not provided in a manner that tracks directly to the example content for RFP Section L provided in Appendix C.

Subfactor: Software

The Government will evaluate the proposal to determine the offeror's ability to implement a disciplined and institutionalized systems and software engineering approach to successfully design, develop, integrate, validate and verify, manufacture, and sustain the *<program>* system as defined by the SRD performance capability requirements and documented in the system specification. The software development capability will be evaluated to assess the offeror's understanding of software development; ability to implement critical technical processes and approaches/plans; ability to efficiently and effectively manage and integrate the development program; and capability to manage, develop, and integrate the software elements required to satisfy the performance requirements. This subfactor is intended to evaluate proposed processes and approaches for software development and integration, sustainment planning, software deliverables and technical data, and license rights.

Measure of Merit: This subfactor is met when the offeror's proposal demonstrates [note: tailor from these as applicable]:

a. An effective software design, development, integration, verification, and sustainment process, tailored from a company standard development approach, that is fully defined in the proposed SDP, integrated into the IMP and IMS, and reflected in the SOW.

b. An appropriate software life cycle model.

c. A sound approach for planning development blocks/increments.

d. A preliminary CS&S architecture that identifies all computing system elements and all software components to be developed, reused, and integrated.

e. A sound approach to identifying and managing computer system and software risks.

f. A realistic estimate of the size of the proposed software development and integration effort, considering expected software size growth during development, proposed software reuse, proposed modification to existing software, proposed use of COTS/NDI products, and other software development and integration risks.

g. A sound technical approach to the requirements process that provides adequate traceability, aligns requirements with capability blocks/increments, and minimizes rework.

h. A sound approach for software activity planning and statusing, including the use of software metrics.

i. An effective approach for applying EVM to software.

j. Proprietary rights and intellectual property considerations that are appropriate and acceptable based on the expected operational and support approaches for software.

k. Proper attention to safety and security concerns, including safety critical functions, fault tolerance, and redundancy management.

l. An acceptable quality management and product control approach that addresses software quality management, software quality assurance, defect control (software problem reporting, tracking, and resolution), peer reviews, software configuration management, and documentation.

m. A sound approach for software sustainment planning.

n. A consistent approach to addressing software size, technical content, development effort (cost), and schedule throughout the proposal (for example, ensure the size of the software proposed in the technical volume is reflected in the cost volume).

o. Realistic assumptions for software engineering productivity.

p. Commitment to identify and correct development process weaknesses.

q. Compatibility of the proposed software development processes with the proposed software effort, schedule, and performance baselines.

r.   Appropriate integration of software engineering and systems engineering.

s.   An acceptable approach to ensure that adequate personnel, development stations, integration labs, and other needed facilities will be available in the required quantities and locations to support the proposed development.

t.   An acceptable approach for testing/verifying GFS well prior to need, and an understanding that such software is provided "as-is."

u.   An acceptable approach for managing software suppliers, including flow-down of performance and process requirements, use of common development environments, balance of risk and supplier contract type, and approach to insight, communication, and control.

v.   An acceptable approach for organizational standards and procedures, training, technology assessment and transition, and organizational process management.

Appendix E
Software Contracting Considerations

E.1   Background

There are a number of pitfalls to be avoided when contracting for software intensive systems. For example, failure of Government furnished software could render the Government responsible for subsequent failures on the part of the contractor. Another example is applying an improper type of contract for software development. Yet another is the establishment of contract incentives which do not emphasize desired aspects of contractor performance, such as emphasizing speed of delivery at the expense of software quality. These and other contracting issues related to software are addressed here to ensure contracts are structured to avoid undue risk associated with Government furnished software, and to provide incentives for the software developer to achieve performance, cost, schedule and life-cycle support goals.

E.2   Government Furnished Software

Acquisition organizations must exercise extreme caution when providing software as GFE/GFP/GFI to the development contractor. This includes software tools to support the development process.

Air Force policy for providing software as GFE/GFP was previously contained in AFR 800-14, Para 3-14c, which stated: "Government provided software tools (for example: compilers, emulators, pre-processors) will not be used to support contracted development efforts unless those tools are made available for evaluation by prospective vendors prior to being placed on contract, and Government provided support for those tools is available." While AFR 800-14 has been rescinded, this guidance is still sound.

Programs have in some cases used Government furnished software tools because of expected risk reduction and cost and schedule savings. In some instances, expected benefits from the use of GFP/GFE have not been realized. This may be due to the technology being immature, attempting to use the software for other than its original intended purpose, or other factors. In all known instances, the Government has been held responsible for any impacts to the system development when Government furnished tools did not perform as expected.

The preferred approach is to specify the requirements in performance terms, and then require the development contractor to select his own tools based upon his analysis of those tools and software available in the marketplace. This approach places the responsibility on the development contractor to assess the maturity and product quality of candidate software packages, and to arrange for life cycle support, as required, to satisfy contract requirements.

E.2.1   Software Co-Developed by the Government

Some recent programs have incorporated Government software through a co-development arrangement where a Government entity enters into a type of subcontract or partnering agreement with the prime contractor. In this case, the Government entity is treated as a subcontractor during the source selection, and personnel working for the Government entity are prohibited from participating in the source selection except through contractor discussions. Strengths, weaknesses, and risks associated with the Government entity's software development capabilities must be assessed just as for any other proposed software developer.

E.2.2   Steps for Dealing with Government Furnished Software (GFS)

In general, if the Government provides GFS to the contractor, it is difficult to hold the contractor liable for performance. The Government is normally responsible for the condition and suitability for use of the GFS. As a result, in cases where it is advantageous or necessary to provide GFS, if possible the contract should be structured so that the Government is not held responsible for the performance, support, or maintenance of the software by providing the GFS "as is" in accordance with contract clause **FAR 52.245-1** "Government Property."

The incorporation of such software should be addressed as part of the system acquisition and development similar to software from any other source, starting with the system architecture. Apply all applicable acquisition management processes to GFS in development or being modified. Also, establish clearly in the contract the responsibilities of each party in dealing with GFS, especially in the case where GFS may contribute to a failure to meet contract requirements. If there is intent to provide GFS to the contractor, it should be brought to the attention of the contracting officer during acquisition planning to ensure that all aspects of responsibility and liability for GFS are addressed in the RFP and resulting contract.

FAR 52.245-1, Government Property clause

(d) *Government-furnished property.*

    (1) The Government shall deliver to the Contractor the Government-furnished property described in this contract. The Government shall furnish related data and information needed for the intended use of the property. The warranties of suitability of use and timely delivery of Government-furnished property do not apply to property acquired or fabricated by the Contractor as contractor-acquired property and subsequently transferred to another contract with this Contractor.

    (2) The delivery and/or performance dates specified in this contract are based upon the expectation that the Government-furnished property will be suitable for contract performance and will be delivered to the Contractor by the dates stated in the contract.

        (i) If the property is not delivered to the Contractor by the dates stated in the contract, the Contracting Officer shall, upon the Contractor's timely written request, consider an equitable adjustment to the contract.

        (ii) In the event property is received by the Contractor, or for Government-furnished property after receipt and installation, in a condition not suitable for its intended use, the Contracting Officer shall, upon the Contractor's timely written request, advise the Contractor on a course of action to remedy the problem. Such action may include repairing, replacing, modifying, returning, or otherwise disposing of the property at the Government's expense. Upon completion of the required action(s), the Contracting Officer shall consider an equitable adjustment to the contract (see also paragraph (f)(1)(ii)(A) of this clause).

        (iii) The Government may, at its option, furnish property in an "as-is" condition. The Contractor will be given the opportunity to inspect such property prior to the property being provided. In such cases, the Government makes no warranty with respect to the serviceability and/or suitability of the property for contract performance. Any repairs, replacement, and/or refurbishment shall be at the Contractor's expense.

[end of clause]

E.3   Intellectual Property

The material in this section is adapted from "Guidebook for Acquisition of Naval Software Intensive Systems," Version 1.0 (Draft), developed by Office of the Assistant Secretary of the Navy (Research, Development and Acquisition), ASN(RD&A), May 2008.

Acquiring more than "standard" rights for commercial software is often cost-prohibitive, but the cost must be carefully weighed against any potential benefits to the Government. Program offices need to exercise care to ensure that the context into which COTS items are placed is defined with sufficient rights so that the Government can pursue alternative solutions for future upgrades. That is, the interfaces to the COTS products must be available to the Government. Also, while offerors may appear to be providing all COTS, or may make grand open architecture claims, this section still applies to whatever software is required to configure and integrate these COTS items into a system that operates as required. Such software includes so-called "glue" code that enables integration, scripts that configure the COTS and the operating systems, database (e.g., Structured Query Language (SQL)) code that drives the COTS, and whatever else is needed to make it all work.

E.3.1   Overview

Intellectual property deals with the rights associated with the products produced by contractors, including the various software products. The establishment of Intellectual Property (IP) terms and conditions is a critical aspect of any software intensive systems acquisition activity. Without the proper data rights, programs will not be able to legally use, modify, and support their deliverables the way they want or need, regardless of what other portions of a contract appear to say.

It is critical, legally speaking, that the RFP and the offeror's response distinguish between commercial and noncommercial software. Commercial software is set forth in <u>DFARS 252.227-7014(a)</u> as software developed or regularly used for non-governmental purposes and either 1) sold, leased, or licensed to the public; 2) offered for sale, lease, or license to the public; 3) doesn't meet the two prior conditions but will be available for commercial sale, lease, or license in time to satisfy the delivery requirements of this contract; or 4) meets any of the prior three conditions and would require only minor modification to meet the requirements of the contract. Commercial computer software should be acquired under the licenses customarily provided to the public unless such licenses are inconsistent with federal procurement law or do not otherwise satisfy user needs. For example, a commercial computer software license may be modified to refer to federal law instead of a particular state law or modified to request source code in order to support a program requirement to integrate the software into an existing system. Noncommercial software is any software that does not meet the description of commercial software.

For noncommercial software the DFARS includes a standard set of license rights that delineate what the Government can expect, but if these are either 1) not cited, 2) not exercised, or 3) not appropriate for the needs of the Government, then the ability of the Government to take full advantage of the products being acquired will be compromised. It is important to understand that, according to law, the contractor typically owns whatever they develop, such as computer software, computer software documentation, or technical data unless a special works clause is provided in the contract. The Government only receives license rights to use these items. It is therefore crucial that the Government negotiates license rights that are needed for any specific acquisition. The DFARS standard license language provides rights only if the DFARS clauses are placed into the contract. Even then it is possible that the rights might not meet the needs of a particular acquisition. Appropriate CDRLs or other contract deliverables should be prepared for any software that the Government program intends to use, modify or distribute to other contractors. One effective strategy is to include in the RFP a statement based on <u>DFARS 252.227-7017</u> that requires offerors to provide unlimited rights for all products except for those that they explicitly identify.

Beware of software tools that the offeror will use in producing their software. A specific CDRL item should require information on development tools and the IP or warranty on using them to produce the deliverable software product. Details of how these tools are used must also be addressed in the contract for any warranty or future modification or distribution to other Government contractors.

E.3.2   *Assessment of Planned Work – Data Rights Requirements Analysis*

It is the responsibility of the contracting officer to put the proper data rights clauses into the contract, but it is the responsibility of the program office team to provide the contracting officer with a complete assessment of the planned work effort. This assessment should include a determination of the contemplated present uses of the software or other deliverables as well as an assessment of any future uses of the software products or tools used in their production. This assessment is called a "Data Rights Requirements Analysis" (DRRA) and should be conducted prior to contract award using the offeror's response, taking into consideration such factors as multiple site or shared use requirements, and whether the Government's software maintenance philosophy will require the rights to modify or have third parties modify the software or the tools used to modify it.

The results of this analysis should guide the program office in determining the intellectual property and intellectual property rights that it requires the contractor to deliver. If the DRRA determines that the standard data rights clauses do not provide sufficient rights to meet the program's current and future needs, additional rights may be obtained through negotiations with the contractor, usually at additional cost. It is important to perform a trade-off analysis between the additional cost and the benefits realized from obtaining the rights. TABLE E- 1 describes the technical data rights associated with commercial data items, and TABLE E- 2 defines those rights for noncommercial items.

TABLE E- 1. Commercial TD and CS Data Rights Assertion Categories.

Commercial Technical Data (TD) and Computer Software (CS) Data Rights Assertion Categories				
Rights Category	**TD or CS?**	**Criteria for Applying Rights Category**	**Permitted Uses Within Government**	**Permitted Uses Outside Government**
Standard DFARS "7015" Rights	TD only	Default category for all commercial TD (TD pertaining to commercial items) except those qualifying for Unlimited Rights	Unlimited; except may not be used for manufacture	Only with contractor's written permission or for emergency repair/overhaul.
Unlimited Rights (UR)	TD only	Commercial TD that: 1) has previously been provided to the Government or is already publicly available without restrictions; 2) is "form, fit and function"; 3) is a correction to TD previously delivered to the Government; 4) has been provided to the Government with UR from a prior contract; or, 5) is necessary for operation, maintenance, installation or training	Unlimited; no restrictions	
Standard Commercial License	CS only	Default rights category for all commercial CS	As specified in the license customarily offered to the public. DoD must negotiate for any specialized needs, or if any of the license terms are unacceptable to the Government.	
Specifically Negotiated License Rights	Both TD and CS	Mutual agreement of the parties; should be used whenever the standard categories do not meet both parties' needs.	As negotiated by the parties; however, by statute, the Government cannot accept less than the minimum standard 7015 rights in commercial TD.	

TABLE E- 2. Non-Commercial TD and CS Data Rights Assertion Categories.

Non-Commercial Technical Data (TD) and Computer Software (CS) Data Rights Assertion Categories				
Rights Category	**TD or CS?**	**Criteria for Applying Rights Category**	**Permitted Uses Within Government**	**Permitted Uses Outside Government**
Unlimited Rights (UR)	TD and CS	Applies to: 1) TD/CS that is Developed exclusively at Government expense; 2) TD that is test data; 3) TD that is form, fit and function data; 4) TD that is necessary for operation, maintenance or training; 5) Corrections or changes to TD/CS previously delivered to the Government; 6) TD/CS otherwise publicly available; 7) CS Documentation deliverables; and, 8) TD/CS whose GPR have expired.	Unlimited; no restrictions. Note: If a third party copyright is asserted in TD/CS that is delivered with UR, under DFARS 227.7203-9 the delivering contractor must grant or obtain for the Government license rights that permit the Government to reproduce, perform or display the software or documentation; distribute copies; and, through the right to modify data, prepare derivative works. If the contractor does not obtain an appropriate license for the Government, then the contractor should not incorporate the unlicensed copyrighted material into the deliverable TD/CS without the Contracting Officer's written approval	
Government Purpose Rights (GPR)	TD and CS	Development with mixed funding	Unlimited; no restrictions	For "Government Purposes"; no commercial use. Must have recipient sign a Non-Disclosure Agreement (NDA)
Limited Rights (LR)	TD only	Development exclusively at private expense	Unlimited; except may not be used for manufacture	Emergency repair/overhaul; evaluation by foreign government; may also disclose subject to a prohibition on any further disclosure after notifying the asserting contractor
Restricted Rights (RR)	CS only	Development exclusively at private expense	Government may: 1) Use on one computer at a time; 2) Transfer to another Government entity (transferor must destroy all copies); 3) Make minimum backup copies; and 4) Modify, provided there is no release or disclosure outside Government.	Emergency repair/overhaul (w/NDA). Support contractors may use (w/NDA).
Prior Government Rights (DFARS 252.227- 028)	Both TD and CS	Whenever Government has previously acquired rights in the deliverable TD/CS.	Same as under previous contract	
Specifically Negotiated License Rights (SNLR)	Both TD and CS	Mutual agreement of the parties; use whenever the standard categories do not meet both parties' needs	As negotiated by the parties; however, must not be less than LR in TD and must not be less than RR in CS	
SBIR Data Rights	Both TD and CS	Whenever TD/CS is generated under a SBIR contract, regardless of funding. SBIR Data Rights expire five years after completion of the SBIR project from which such TD/CS were generated.	Within Government, use and disclosure is unlimited	Cannot release or disclose SBIR data outside of Government, other than support services contractors, except: 1) As expressly permitted by the contractor; 2) For evaluation purposes; or, 3) For emergency repair or overhaul. When disclosed outside Government, an NDA is required.

E.3.3   DRRA Principles

The following principles should be considered when performing a data rights assessment:

a. Data rights issues are complex and require careful examination of the program's requirements and overall "fit" within the enterprise. Establishing the data rights strategy for a program requires expert guidance from Government attorneys and the contracting officer to determine the best strategy.

b. Subject matter experts should be used to review program data rights requirements. Strategy development should involve software and architecture experts, an intellectual property lawyer, a contracting officer and the program manager.

c. It is typically very expensive to acquire broader data rights or to create additional options for software maintenance after the initial contract is in place. Inadequate data rights typically result in substantial additional cost to acquire the required rights or having only one option for software maintenance: sole source procurement to the original developer of the software. Sole sources have little incentive to offer lowest cost.

d. Insufficient data rights prevent the Government from using deliverables in the most optimal way.

e. Data rights will impact maintenance over 30 or more years of a system's life.

f. Programs should perform a Business Case Analysis (BCA) as a part of assessing the IP needs to determine whether obtaining the desired rights is the correct business decision.

E.3.4   DRRA Considerations

A DRRA should address the following issues:

a. Is this a new or existing procurement?

b. What type of procurement or assistance vehicle is/will be involved (Federal Acquisition Regulations (FAR)/DFARS contract, grant or cooperative agreement).

c. Does the Government already have data rights in existing software or other deliverables that permit the Government to leverage (i.e., modify and/or enhance) that existing software for this new contracting effort (including necessary architecture/design/interface documentation)?

d. What clauses already exist regarding data rights?

e. What are the benefits of broader data rights clauses? For example, will acquiring more than restricted/limited rights impact procurement cost without providing value?

f. Will one of the standard DFARS levels of data rights ("unlimited," "Government purpose" or "restricted/limited") be acceptable, or do the data rights need to be specifically tailored for this procurement?

g. Does the number of anticipated changes to the software and the required response time for those changes warrant the possible additional cost or fewer bidders on the procurement?

h. Will the Government obtain at least Government purpose rights (GPR)? If not, is the asset isolated at the lowest component level? If not, is it non-critical? If not, what is the justification for less than GPR?

i.   Has the program identified potential components and artifacts that can be provided to the offerors as Government furnished information (GFI)?

j.   Does the Government have the right to provide the information to third parties? If not, should the Government negotiate a license for this right?

k.   What is the likelihood that the Government will perform the software maintenance (i.e., error corrections and enhancements) organically?

l.   What is the likelihood that the software maintenance will be competed and awarded to a third party?

m.   Might there be any situations that would require licensing outside the Federal Government (e.g., FMS or commercial)?

n.   Does the Government require the rights to modify the deliverables now or in the future (modifications include updates, corrections and enhancements)?

o.   Will the Government need special tools to be able to modify the deliverables?

p.   Do the components to be acquired fit within an existing, approved Government architecture, or can they be easily modified to fit into an approved architecture? Does the Government have sufficient rights to perform this modification?

q.   Does the Government need to maintain configuration control over the deliverables? If so, the Government needs to obtain sufficient license terms to perform this maintenance.

When performing the DRRA, it is important to address both long-term as well as short-term needs, since software could be in use for 30 or more years.

After the DRRA has been conducted, the program office team can determine if the standard data rights clauses provide the rights that the contractor and the Government need to accomplish the stated objectives. If additional rights are required, the contracting officer can enter into negotiations with the contractor to acquire such rights.

E.3.5   Commercial-Off-The-Shelf and Open Source Software

Currently, the DFARS require the identification of noncommercial software to which the Government has less than unlimited rights. It is also necessary for acquisitions to require identification of any commercial software (such as COTS, open source, "Freeware") that are or have the potential to be a part of the software items to be delivered in fulfillment of contract requirements. In particular, some open source license terms may prove to be too restrictive for Government use. Contractors also need to identify the license terms of any software tools or libraries used to build the software products, to allow the Government an opportunity to plan for system sustainment.

In the case of open source software that is adapted for use in the defense environment, the development contractor should typically remove it from the open source environment and assume configuration control of the product as if it were developed code. Modifications and enhancements made to open source software for defense purposes should generally not become public domain.

E.3.6   Other Sources of Information about Intellectual Property Rights

The FAR and DFARS is the primary source of information regarding data rights. Applicable FAR/DFARS intellectual property/technical data/software provisions:

a. FAR 52.227-11, Patent Rights – Retention by the Contractor (Short Form).

b. FAR 52.227-12, Patent Rights – Retention by the Contractor (Long Form).

c. DFARS 252.227-7013, Rights in Technical Data – Noncommercial Items.

d. DFARS 252.227-7014, Rights in Noncommercial Computer Software and Noncommercial Computer Software Documentation.

e. DFARS 252.227-7015, Technical Data – Commercial Items.

f. DFARS 252.227-7016, Rights in Bid or Proposal Information.

g. DFARS 252.227-7017, Identification and Assertion of Use, Release, or Disclosure Restrictions.

h. DFARS 252.227-7018, Rights in Non-commercial Technical Data and Computer Software – Small Business Innovation Research (SBIR) Program.

i. DFARS 252.227-7019, Validation of Asserted Restrictions – Computer Software.

j. DFARS 252.227-7020, Rights in Special Works.

k. DFARS 252.227-7025, Limitations on the Use or Disclosure of Government Furnished Information Marked with Restrictive Legends.

l. DFARS 252.227-7027, Deferred Ordering of Technical Data or Computer Software.

m. DFARS 252.227-7028, Technical Data or Computer Software Previously Delivered to Government.

n. DFARS 252.227-7030, Technical Data – Withholding of Payment.

o. DFARS 252.227-7037, Validation of Restrictive Markings on Technical Data.

FAR/DFARS materials can be accessed at: *http://www.acq.osd.mil/dpap/dars/index.html*.

E.4   Contract Types for Software Development

Contract type is an important consideration in acquisition of software intensive systems, and is normally determined during formation of the acquisition strategy. The two major contract types typically used for weapon system acquisition are cost reimbursement and fixed price.

Fixed price contracts are best applied in situations where development risk is small and requirements are stable and well understood. Limited development risk allows the contractor to cover the risk at a reasonable price. Requirements should be well understood so the Government does not have to constantly modify the contract to meet the needs of the user. Weapon system software development does not typically fit this scenario. This is because even though system level performance requirements may be known at the outset, the complete set of software level requirements may not be defined for months (perhaps years) later, once the development has progressed down through system and subsystem designs, where an adequate understanding of the required software performance has been established.

Cost reimbursement type contacts are much more common for software intensive weapon system development. Cost reimbursement type contracts can be implemented with fixed or variable fees as follows:

a. Cost Plus Fixed Fee (CPFF), which provides a fixed fee dollar amount but no incentives for cost control, schedule, or performance.

b. Cost Plus Incentive Fee (CPIF), which relies on objective incentives for cost control that are defined in the contract. There are no incentives for performance or schedule.

c. Cost Plus Award Fee (CPAF), which provides for subjective incentives for management, cost, performance, and schedule. The incentives can be revised periodically to emphasize different, important aspects of contract performance (e.g. design at the beginning of the contract and operational test performance and support at the end).

The basic characteristics of each contract type are determined in each case by the specific wording of the contract (most notably in the special provisions), so generalizations may not always hold. It is advisable to consult with the contracting officer to understand the characteristics of a specific contract. Nevertheless, TABLE E- 3 contrasts some observed general characteristics of fixed price vs. cost reimbursement type contracts:

E.5   Software Contract Line Items (CLINs)

The overall CLIN structure for the program must first be determined by working with the contracting officer, based on contract type and program objectives. Separate CLINs can be established for software if it is a separate deliverable under the contract. Identifying software as a contract line item in the model contract included in the RFP ensures that software has appropriate visibility and accountability, and aids in the reporting of software cost. Another consideration is the method of "selling off" the CLIN, for example, through completion of DT&E testing. The program office must ensure that requirements sell-off involves all relevant components, both hardware and software.

CDRL templates for Software Resources Data Reports are also available.

E.6   Critical Processes

The Government ensures its rights to expect the contractor to perform to his critical processes by placing essential development processes on contract. The IMP is the vehicle to accomplish this, together with the contractor's SDP, which contains descriptions of these processes.

E.7   Coordination with Defense Contract Management Agency (DCMA)

DCMA can play a vital role in monitoring the execution of the development processes through MOAs or similar instruments. The program office and DCMA should jointly define the DCMA role in the program, starting in the RFP preparation phase.

TABLE E- 3. Contract Type Comparison.

Characteristic	Fixed Price/Firm Fixed-Price (FFP)	Cost Reimbursement or Fixed-Price Incentive (FPI)
Contractor provided Software Cost Estimates	Estimated at higher confidence levels	Historically estimated at lower confidence levels
Contractor provided Software Schedule Estimates	Estimated at higher confidence levels	Historically estimated at lower confidence levels
Requirements compliance	Mandatory	Best Effort
Requirements wording	Extremely precise or a specific product description, less functional based	Precise but less specific, more top-level or functional based
Visibility into actual cost incurred	None	Required at specific WBS levels
Visibility into earned value status	Possible	Required at specific WBS levels
Cost Overruns	Borne by Contractor	Borne by Government for CPFF Partially borne by Government for CPIF, CPAF, or FPI
Process compliance (e.g. SDP)	Little or no Government emphasis/insight	More emphasis
Schedule compliance	Schedule compliance inherent and enforceable through the contract. Can include additional incentives for schedule performance.	Schedule compliance inherent and enforceable through the contract. Award fee or performance incentives can provide additional incentives for schedule performance.
Requirements flexibility	Strictly controlled. Minimal flexibility. Contract changes may be costly.	Spec and lower level requirements more flexibly implemented. Requirements changes are still costly.
Constructive changes	Not allowed	Not allowed

Appendix F
Computer Systems and Software
Criteria for Technical Reviews

This appendix defines CS&S related criteria for the typical systems and software-engineering technical reviews. It provides an overview of the objective of each review, as well as inputs and outputs. The reviews addressed here include:

a. CS&S Support to the System Requirements Review (SRR).

b. CS&S Support to the System Functional Review (SFR).

c. Software Specification Review (SSR).

d. CS&S Support to the System Preliminary Design Review (PDR).

e. Software Preliminary Design Review (PDR).

f. CS&S Support to the System Critical Design Review (CDR).

g. Software Critical Design Review (CDR).

h. Software Test Readiness Review (TRR).

i. CS&S Support to the System Test Readiness Review (TRR).

j. Software Functional Configuration Audit (FCA).

k. CS&S Support to the System Functional Configuration Audit (FCA).

l. CS&S Support to the System Verification Review (SVR).

m. Software Physical Configuration Audit (PCA).

n. CS&S Support to the System Physical Configuration Audit (PCA).

Note on technical review discipline: Issues frequently arise that can adversely impact the effectiveness of technical reviews. Late submission of inadequate documentation in an effort to meet an aggressively scheduled review typically leads to numerous unresolved technical issues and a long list of action items. Entrance criteria for all reviews should include timely availability of complete and correct review documentation. In addition, technical reviews should not be considered "closed" until all resulting technical issues and action items are resolved to the satisfaction of the review chairs.

F.1   CS&S Support to the System Requirements Review (SRR)

The SRR is conducted to ascertain progress in defining system technical requirements. This review determines the direction and progress of the systems engineering effort and the degree of convergence upon a balanced and complete configuration. It is normally held during Technology Development, but may be repeated after the start of System Development and Demonstration to clarify the contractor's understanding of redefined or new user requirements. [From the Defense Acquisition Guidebook.]

The SRR is a multi-disciplined technical review to ensure that the system under review can proceed into the System Development and Demonstration phase, and that all system requirements and performance requirements derived from the Initial Capabilities Document or draft Capability Development Document are defined and are consistent with cost (program budget), schedule (program schedule), risk, and other system constraints. Generally this review assesses the system requirements as captured in the system specification, and ensures that the system requirements are consistent with the preferred system solution as well as available technologies resulting from the Technology Development phase. Of critical importance to this review is an understanding of the program technical risk inherent in the system specification and in the System Development and Demonstration Phase Systems Engineering Plan. Determining an acceptable level of risk is key to a successful review.

The SRR is essential to fully establish, understand and define the CS&S requirements in the system requirements definition process. For systems involving significant exploitation of CS&S technology integral to the system requirements and architecture with follow-on CS&S development, senior computer systems and software engineers should be involved in the SRR process.

The input and output criteria identified below should be scoped in a manner consistent with the acquisition concept. For example in a Waterfall model the requirements should be defined at the entrance to this process block whereas in a block/incremental development acquisition the requirements may evolve with each block/increment in the development. Therefore multiple SRRs may occur in a block/incremental development acquisition.

F.1.1   Inputs/Entry Criteria
a. Draft system specification with CS&S performance (specific and implied) requirements, including CS&S verification requirements.
b. CS&S architectures as integral to the system architecture.
c. Candidate CS&S technologies identified.
d. CS&S coverage in the draft LCMP and IMP.

F.1.2   Outputs (Exit Criteria)
a. CS&S requirements are defined in the complete draft system specification, including specific verification requirements.
b. Identification and assessment of key CS&S technologies to be exploited/applied, including a strategy and process to mature the higher risk technologies.
c. CS&S requirements are defined in the draft interface specifications and control documents.
d. CS&S risks (including those related to cost, schedule, and performance) have been identified and mitigation plans have been developed.
e. CS&S demonstrations and prototyping plans are defined.
f. Preliminary software development processes are defined and documented.
g. Initial software development size, effort, and schedule estimates are defined.
h. Software trade-offs addressing candidate open source software, COTS, reuse, development risks, and architectures are identified and planned.

    i.   Initial allocation of functional requirements to subsystems and to hardware and software are defined.

    j.   Initial S/SEE (i.e. integrated system and software development tool requirements) are defined.

    k.   Software development personnel and training requirements identified.

    l.   Programming languages and architectures, security requirements and, operational and support concepts have been identified.

    m. Preliminary software support data are defined.

F.2   CS&S Support to the System Functional Review (SFR)

The System Functional Review (SFR), sometimes also known as the System Design Review (SDR) is a multi-disciplined technical review to ensure that the system under review can proceed into preliminary design, and that all system requirements and functional performance requirements derived from the Capability Development Document are defined and are consistent with cost (program budget), schedule (program schedule), risk, and other system constraints. Generally this review assesses the system functional requirements as captured in system specifications (functional baseline), and ensures that all required system performance is fully decomposed and defined in the functional baseline. System performance may be decomposed and traced to lower-level subsystem functionality that may define hardware and software requirements. The SFR determines whether the systems functional definition is fully decomposed to a low level, and whether the IPT is prepared to start preliminary design. [From the Defense Acquisition Guidebook.]

The SFR further establishes the CS&S requirements and technical considerations. For systems involving significant CS&S technology integral to the system requirements and architecture, this event should involve senior CS&S engineers working as members of a systems engineering team. Lower level subsystems and configuration baselines may be identified and managed as contractor-controlled developmental baselines during the SD&D phase.

As part of the SFR, preliminary CS&S architecture quality attributes (such as modifiability, performance predictability, security, availability, interoperability, and usability) should be reviewed to gain early visibility into critical tradeoffs and design decisions which drive the entire system development effort.

F.2.1   Inputs/Entry Criteria

    a.   All planned reviews are completed, with all CS&S issues resolved or documented with a plan of action to resolve, including a date to reach resolution without program impact.

    b.   Completed system specification with CS&S functional/performance (specific and implied) requirements, including CS&S verification requirements.

    c.   CS&S architectures are defined integral to the system architecture.

    d.   CS&S architecture trade study results.

    e.   Planned CS&S trade studies have been completed.

    f.   Computer system architectures are defined.

g. Subsystems are identified, and computer software configuration item (CSCI) specifications have been drafted.

F.2.2   *Outputs (Exit Criteria)*

a. CS&S requirements defined in the system specification, including specific verification requirements are complete and baselined as part of the system specification.

b. Draft subsystem/allocated functional specifications, including CS&S requirements are completed.

c. Draft contractor-allocated preliminary software requirements specifications (CSCI development specifications), including verification requirements, and interface requirements specifications (IRS) are defined.

d. Development specification tree is defined through subsystems and configuration items, including interface specifications.

e. System/segment design approach is defined, including CS&S architecture.

f. Software development process is defined and reflected in the IMP.

g. Preliminary identification of the S/SEE, i.e. integrated system/software tool set, is defined.

h. CS&S design/development approach is confirmed through analysis, demonstrations, and prototyping.

i. Software process IMP/IMS events, schedule, task definitions, and metrics are defined for the next acquisition phase.

j. Software requirements traceability is defined through the higher tier specifications to the system/subsystem requirement.

k. CS&S risk management strategy and approach is established for the SD&D phase.

l. Preliminary software risk management process is defined and integrated with the system risk management process.

m. All software development work, consistent with the contractor's software development process for the SD&D phase, is defined in the CWBS.

n. Software development estimates for the SD&D phase have been completed.

o. CS&S risks (including those related to cost, schedule, and performance) have been identified and mitigation plans have been developed.

F.3   *Software Specification Review (SSR)*

A Software Specification Review (SSR) is conducted for each CSCI after the SFR, but prior to the initiation of preliminary design for the individual CSCI. The SSR is part of the overall systems engineering process of allocating and formally defining requirements, and must occur after the system/subsystem level hardware/software allocation decisions have been made and the related designs have been completed. The SSR is normally held early in the SD&D phase. Emphasis is on demonstrating the adequacy of the internal development baselines, including the SRS and IRS. The SRR establishes the allocated developmental baseline for the CSCI.

F.3.1   Tasks Performed as a Part of this Review Include

a. Ensuring the SRS performance requirements are feasible, complete, and consistent with the higher level specification requirements (establish traceability).

b. Ensuring all derived requirements have been identified and documented.

c. Ensuring the requirements as stated are testable and measurable.

d. Ensuring there are complete verifiable requirements for all performance requirements, i.e., section 4 is complete and consistent with section 3.

e. Evaluating reserve capacity requirements and scenarios / procedures for measurement.

f. Evaluating agreements on interfaces and boundaries.

g. Evaluating results of functional analyses.

h. Evaluating requirements allocation decisions.

i. Evaluating identified software risks and proposed mitigation methods.

j. Evaluating proposed top level software architecture.

k. Evaluating trade studies and feasibility analyses.

l. Evaluating applicable design constraints.

m. Evaluating applicable human factors considerations.

n. Examining the proposed software development processes.

o. Examining baseline control and configuration management processes.

F.3.2   Inputs/Entry Criteria

a. Draft SRSs and IRSs for all CSCIs to be reviewed.

b. Baselined higher level (system and subsystem) specifications.

c. Software risk management approach and analysis results.

d. Software work packages defined.

e. Draft allocation of requirements to CSCs.

f. SDF formats and tools for establishment and maintenance.

g. Functional analysis results.

h. Software architecture studies and analysis.

F.3.3   Outputs (Exit Criteria)

a. Subsystem and functional issues have been resolved.

b. Computer software subsystem requirements are traceable to higher level requirements.

c. A requirements traceability matrix has been developed identifying how the requirements will be tested, and a section 4 verification requirement exists for each section 3 performance requirement.

d. The set of requirements incorporates the functionality that must be implemented.

e. The internal development baselines (SRS and IRS, if applicable) are established.

f. The software and interface requirements are allocated to CSCIs and CSCs.

g. CS&S risks (including those related to cost, schedule, and performance) have been identified and mitigation plans have been developed.

h. Risks are acceptable and the software development risk management process is defined and integrated with the system risk management process.

i. Requirements are allocated to planned increments (e.g., blocks).

j. Software development schedules, down to and including the software work package schedules, reflect and accommodate contractor selected processes and defined IMP events.

k. Required software integration and test tools and facilities are defined.

l. Life-cycle software support requirements are compatible with, and incorporated into, the system lifecycle resource requirements.

m. Methods are defined to manage and control the growth of the software during the development phase.

n. Metrics to be used by the developer are defined and implemented where applicable.

o. Software development size, staffing, schedule, and cost estimates are updated.

p. The S/SEE requirements are defined.

F.4 CS&S Support to the System Preliminary Design Review (PDR)

The Preliminary Design Review (PDR) is a multi-disciplined technical review to ensure that the system under review can proceed into detailed design, and can meet the stated performance requirements within cost (program budget), schedule (program schedule), risk, and other system constraints. Generally, this review assesses the system preliminary design as captured in performance specifications for each configuration item in the system (allocated baseline), and ensures that each function in the functional baseline has been allocated to one or more system configuration items. Configuration items may consist of hardware and software elements and include such items as airframes, avionics, weapons, crew systems, engines, and trainers/training. [From the Defense Acquisition Guidebook.]

The PDR addresses the CS&S design as part of system and subsystem-level reviews. PDRs form the basis for determining whether a preliminary architecture and design approach for a configuration item are acceptable to start detailed design. These reviews should be held at various levels of the system development, consistent with the specification tree structure, including CIs, aggregations of CIs, subsystem, and system. (The CSCI level PDRs are described below.)

It is incumbent upon development contractors to conduct design review activities which are appropriate for the complexity, life cycle, and degree to which the development is similar to previous developments. Acquisition personnel must ensure that contractor processes entail appropriate design activities, and that adequate customer interface and visibility is maintained. Technically knowledgeable members of the IPT from the acquisition and supporting organizations should participate. For systems involving significant CS&S technology integral to the system design, this event should involve senior CS&S engineers working as members of the IPT. PDR (with its completion criteria) should be accomplished in accordance with plans established and committed to in advance by the contractor in the IMP/IMS and SDP.

At the conclusion of preliminary design, a configuration controlled development specification or description must be complete and ready for use in detailed design. The system level PDR activity is not complete until all software or other lower level PDRs have been completed.

The CS&S requirements specifications should be reviewed for changes and traceability to the preliminary design. Conversely the CS&S design should be reviewed to determine that it fully implements the higher-level functional/design architecture and specified requirements. Impact of changes in requirements should be analyzed for impact to the design. Where necessary, requirements could be reallocated and designs adjusted to be consistent and complete. Analysis should include internal and external interfaces. The verification requirements and procedures should be analyzed for consistency and completeness. Where incremental development is being used, allocation of software requirements to increments (e.g. blocks) should be reviewed for consistency and completeness.

Each PDR ensures the process used to arrive at functional and performance requirements for each configuration item is complete, including trades and allocations; that it demonstrates a balanced and integrated approach; and that it establishes an audit trail from functional baseline to customer requirements, substantiating changes as necessary. The reviews ensure that selected design approaches are confirmed through evaluation of risk mitigation and resolution. Allocation of functional requirements to elements of the software architecture is analyzed for consistency and completeness. The physical architecture and design is assessed to determine adequacy, completeness, and realism of proposed development functional requirements. Finally, the reviews confirm that the integrated system meets functional baseline requirements and that the system preliminary design meets customer requirements.

F.4.1   Inputs/Entry Criteria

    a. System/subsystem functional and performance requirements baseline, including the SRS baseline and any changes since the SSR.

    b. Preliminary system software and CSCI architecture is established and accommodated within the system architecture.

    c. CS&S specified requirements and preliminary design are satisfied or accommodated by the subsystem/system design architecture and approach.

    d. Preliminary CS&S designs are complete and accommodated in the system architecture and design.

    e. CS&S functional performance interface requirements.

    f. CS&S design implementation trade studies.

    g. Make/buy decisions.

    h. Compatibility between the CS&S and all configuration items.

    i. Interchangeability/replaceability decisions baselined.

    j. Scheduled CSCI (CS&S) and subsystem PDRs have been successfully completed per established exit criteria.

k. ECPs including CS&S impacts.

F.4.2   *Outputs/Exit Criteria*

a. Complete preliminary CS&S (CSCI and interface) architectures and designs are established, documented, reviewed, accommodated within the system/subsystem design, and determined to be ready for detailed design.

b. Confirmation that the CS&S specified requirements are satisfied by the design architecture and approach.

c. S/SEE requirements and configuration are defined and internally controlled.

d. Software increments (blocks and builds) are defined and allocated.

e. Open source software, COTS, and reusable software is identified and verified to meet requirements.

f. Software test plans are complete.

g. Software development progress metrics are updated to reflect current development and design status.

h. Software development files are established and maintained current.

i. Software development estimates (effort and schedule) are updated.

j. Life-cycle software support requirements are updated.

k. CS&S risks (including those related to cost, schedule, and performance) have been identified and mitigation plans have been developed.

l. Approval is granted to start detailed subsystem / system design.

F.5   *Software Preliminary Design Review (PDR)*

The PDR forms the basis for determining whether a preliminary architecture and design approach for a configuration item is acceptable to start detailed design. This section provides guidance concerning typical content which should be expected in software preliminary design review activities, as well as completion criteria to be satisfied. The objectives of the software PDR are very similar to those defined for the system PDR above, except that the product being addressed is at the software level rather than the system/subsystem level.

At the conclusion of software preliminary design, a configuration controlled development specification or description must be complete and ready for use in detailed design. For complex systems, the system level PDR activities should be concluded only after completion of all software or other lower level reviews and before detailed design begins.

Each PDR ensures the process used to arrive at functional and performance requirements for each configuration item is complete including trades and allocations; that it demonstrates a balanced and integrated approach; and that it establishes an audit trail from functional baseline to customer requirements, substantiating changes as necessary. The reviews ensure that selected design approaches are confirmed through evaluation of risk mitigation and resolution. The physical architecture and design is assessed to determine adequacy, completeness, and realism of proposed development functional requirements. Higher level configuration items (integration and interface) are assessed to ensure they satisfy their portion of the functional baseline. Finally, the reviews confirm that the integrated system meets functional baseline requirements and that the system preliminary design meets customer requirements.

F.5.1   *Inputs (Entry Criteria)*

    a. System/subsystem functional and performance requirements baseline, including the SRS baseline.

    b. Preliminary CSCI architecture.

    c. Preliminary CS&S designs.

    d. CS&S functional performance interface requirements.

    e. CS&S design implementation trade studies.

    f. Make/buy decisions.

    g. Compatibility between all configuration items.

    h. Interchangeability/replaceability decisions baselined.

F.5.2   *Outputs (Exit Criteria)*

    a. Software risk management process is defined and implemented, consistent with the overall risk management process.

    b. Software architectural level design is established.

    c. S/SEE requirements and configuration are defined and internally controlled.

    d. Preliminary software design is defined and documented.

    e. Software requirements baseline is verified to satisfy system/subsystem functional and performance requirements baseline (complete or approved).

    f. Software increments (blocks and builds) are defined and allocated.

    g. Preliminary Interface Control Document (ICDs) are defined.

    h. Software metrics are defined and implemented.

    i. Software test plan is defined and documented.

    j. Initial evaluation of open source software, commercial off-the-shelf (COTS), and reusable software has been completed.

    k. Life-cycle software support requirements are updated.

    l. Software development processes are defined and implemented.

    m. Software development estimates are updated.

    n. Preliminary allocated baseline is ready for start of detailed design for each software item.

    o. CS&S risks (including those related to cost, schedule, and performance) have been identified and mitigation plans have been developed.

    p. Software item is approved to start detailed design.

F.6 *CS&S Support to the System Critical Design Review (CDR)*

The CDR is a multi-disciplined technical review to ensure that the system under review can proceed into system fabrication, demonstration, and test; and can meet the stated performance requirements within cost (program budget), schedule (program schedule), risk, and other system constraints. Generally this review assesses the system final design as captured in product specifications for each configuration item in the system (product baseline), and ensures that each product in the product baseline has been captured in the detailed design documentation. Product specifications for hardware enable the fabrication of configuration items, and may include production drawings. Product specifications for software (e.g., Software Design Documents) enable coding of a Computer Software Configuration Item. Configuration items may consist of hardware and software elements, and include items such as airframe, avionics, weapons, crew systems, engines, and trainers/training. [From the Defense Acquisition Guidebook]

CDRs should be accomplished at various levels of the system development, consistent with the specification tree structure, including critical items, aggregations of critical items, subsystem, and system. CDRs should address the CS&S design as part of the subsystem and system-level critical (detail) design reviews (the software CSCI-level CDRs are described below).

The CS&S requirements specifications should be reviewed for changes and traceability to the detailed design. Conversely the CS&S design should be reviewed to determine if it fully implements the higher-level functional/design architecture and specified requirements. Impact of changes in requirements should be analyzed for impact to the design. Where necessary, requirements should be reallocated and designs adjusted to be consistent and complete. Analysis should include internal and external interfaces. The verification requirements and procedures should be analyzed for consistency and completeness.

Allocation of functional requirements to software configuration items, components, and units should be analyzed for consistency and completeness. Where incremental development is being used, allocation of software requirements to increments (e.g. blocks) should be reviewed for consistency and completeness.

F.6.1 *Inputs (Entry Criteria)*

a. Software requirements developmental (contractor) baseline(s) confirmed to satisfy system/subsystem requirements baselines.

b. Software increments planned and defined, e.g. blocks, including requirements allocated to the planned and defined increments.

c. Software system architectural level design established.

d. Confirmation that the CS&S specified requirements are satisfied by the design architecture and approach.

e. Scheduled CSCI (software) and subsystem CDRs have been successfully completed per established exit criteria.

f. Complete detail level CS&S designs.

g. CS&S specifications, including changes since PDR.

h. ECPs including CS&S impacts.

F.6.2   Outputs (Exit Criteria)

a. S/SEE, the integrated software development toolset, is implemented and ready to support the code and unit test phase.

b. Complete detail level CS&S designs are reviewed and determined to be ready for implementation.

c. Confirmation that the CS&S specified requirements are satisfied by the design architecture and approach.

d. Software (CSCI) detail level design is established.

e. Software test descriptions are complete.

f.   Draft software test procedures are complete.

g. Detailed software design and interface descriptions are complete.

h. Software development progress metrics are being used and are updated to reflect current development and design status.

i.   Software development files are established and maintained current.

j.   Updated evaluation of open source software, commercial off-the-shelf (COTS), and reusable software has been completed.

k. Software development estimates are updated.

l.   CSCI interface control documents are defined in the developmental baseline.

m. Life-cycle software support requirements are updated.

n. CS&S risks (including those related to cost, schedule, and performance) have been identified and mitigation plans have been developed.

o. Approval is granted to start CSCI code and unit test.

F.7   Software Critical Design Review (CDR)

Software CDRs should be performed at the CSCI level for software intensive systems. The primary purpose of the software CSCI CDR is to determine if the completed detailed design meets the specified requirements established in the pertinent developmental baseline (functional/performance) specification, and the design is complete and ready to be implemented (i.e., coded and unit tested).

The SRSs should be reviewed for changes and traceability to the completed detailed design. Impact of changes in requirements should be analyzed for impact to the detailed software design. Where necessary, software requirements should be reallocated and designs adjusted to be consistent and complete. Analysis should include internal and external interfaces. The verification requirements and procedures should be analyzed for consistency and completeness.

Software CSCI designs should be analyzed for consistency with the CS&S design architecture and interfaces with other elements of the system design. Where incremental development is being used, the CSCI design should be reviewed for completeness and consistency for each increment scheduled to be completed. Design allocations between and among the planned increments should be analyzed and reviewed.

F.7.1   Inputs (Entry Criteria)

a. Software CSCI requirements developmental (contractor) baseline(s) confirmed to satisfy system/subsystem requirements baselines.

b. Software CSCI increments planned and defined, e.g. blocks, including requirements allocated to the planned and defined increments.

c. Software system architectural level design established.

d. Confirmation that the CS&S specified requirements are satisfied by the design architecture and approach.

e. Current software CSCI metrics tracking development status and progress.

f. Complete detail level CS&S designs.

g. CS&S specifications, including changes since PDR.

h. ECPs including CS&S impacts.

F.7.2   Outputs (Exit Criteria)

a. Detail level software CSCI designs are established and reviewed, and are determined to be complete and ready for implementation.

b. Confirmation that the software CSCI requirements, as specified in the contractor developmental baseline specifications, are satisfied by the detailed design description.

c. Software CSCI test descriptions are complete.

d. Draft software CSCI test procedures are complete.

e. Detailed software CSCI design and interface descriptions are complete.

f. Software CSCI development progress metrics are updated to reflect current development and design status.

g. Software CSCI development files are established and maintained current.

h. Software CSCI development estimates are updated as part of the balance and control process.

i. CS&S risks (including those related to cost, schedule, and performance) have been identified and mitigation plans have been developed.

F.8   Software Test Readiness Review (TRR)

The CS&S TRR is a software-only activity performed to ensure the software is ready to enter CSCI level qualification testing.

The TEMP, or its functional equivalent, is the basis for the software test planning and readiness activity leading to the TRR. The developer's software development process is the other key input to TRR planning. Key features and subsystems, interfaces with existing or planned systems required for mission accomplishment, identification of critical system characteristics, explicit technical performance measurement results against user defined requirements, developmental test schedules that include statutory tests, and other information that is required to fully design the system must all be considered as elements of TRR planning. The test readiness activity must ensure all of these items are included where software is a part of the subsystem/system.

Typical documents reviewed during this activity may include the SRS, IRS, test plans and descriptions, Computer System Operators Manual (CSOM), Software Users Manual (SUM), and the Computer Systems Diagnostic Manual (CSDM). Other items that may be addressed include lower level test and integration results; CSCI test procedures; other documentation updates; software problem reports; and software test tools, facilities, and schedules including sufficient resources availability (time on the test facilities) over the planned testing period.

During the TRR, test procedures are evaluated for compliance with the SRS, IRS, TEMP or its functional equivalent, and other documentation as applicable. Results of lower level testing accomplished to date are reviewed to ensure all functional and performance requirements have been satisfied (no significant deficiencies exist in the product being tested). Open problem reports against the product being tested, the process used to develop the product, or the environment being used in the test are reviewed and assured to be acceptable. The TRR is successful when it is determined the software test procedures and the lower level test results form a satisfactory basis for proceeding to CSCI level and system testing.

F.8.1   Inputs/Entry Criteria

a. The requirements being tested (applicable SRS and IRS, or subsets) are identified.

b. Traceability of test requirements to the SRS and IRSs is established.

c. All CSCI level test procedures are complete.

d. Objectives of each test are identified.

e. All applicable documentation is complete and controlled (requirements, design, test procedures, version description document.).

f. The method for documenting and dispositioning test anomalies is acceptable.

F.8.2   Outputs (Exit Criteria)

a. Software test descriptions and procedures are defined, verified and baselined.

b. Planned testing is consistent with defined incremental approach including regression testing.

c. All test facilities and resources (including test personnel, lab test stations, hardware, and software) are ready and available to support software testing within the defined schedule.

d. All problem reports applicable to the configuration being tested have been dispositioned.

e. The software being tested and the entire test environment is configuration controlled as applicable.

f. All lower level software testing has been successfully completed and documented.

g. Software metrics show readiness for testing.

h. Software problem report system is defined and implemented.

i. Software test baseline is established and controlled.

j. Software development estimates are updated.

k. Requirements that cannot be adequately tested at the CSCI level (and thus require testing at the subsystem or system levels) are identified.

l. CS&S risks (including those related to cost, schedule, and performance) have been identified and mitigation plans have been developed CS&S support to the system TRR.

The TRR is a multi-disciplined technical review to ensure that the subsystem or system under review is ready to proceed into formal test. The TRR assesses test objectives, test methods and procedures, scope of tests, and safety and confirms that required test resources have been properly identified and coordinated to support planned tests. The TRR verifies the traceability of planned tests to program requirements and user needs. The TRR determines the completeness of test procedures and their compliance with test plans and descriptions. The TRR assesses the system under review for development maturity, cost/schedule effectiveness, and risk to determine readiness to proceed to formal testing. In addition to adequate planning and management, to be effective the program manager should follow-up with the outcomes of the TRR. Test and evaluation is an integral part of the systems engineering processes of Verification and Validation. Test and evaluation should permeate the entire life cycle of an acquisition program. [From the Defense Acquisition Guidebook.]

Any testing required to verify requirements that cannot be adequately verified at the CSCI level must be included in the test plan and reviewed at the system TRR.

During the system TRR, test procedures are evaluated for compliance with the applicable specifications, TEMP or its functional equivalent, and other documentation as applicable. Open problem reports against the product being tested, the process used to develop the product, and the environment being used in the test are reviewed and assured to be acceptable.

F.8.3   Inputs/Entry Criteria

a. The requirements being tested (applicable system/subsystem specifications, SRS and IRS, or subsets) are identified.

b. Traceability of test requirements to the system/subsystem specifications, SRS, and IRS, is established.

c. All lower level tests are complete.

d. All planned CSCI level tests are complete.

e. Objectives of each test are identified.

f. All applicable documentation is complete and controlled (requirements, design, test procedures, version description document).

g. The method for documenting and dispositioning test anomalies is acceptable.

F.8.4   Outputs (Exit Criteria)

a. System test descriptions and procedures are defined, verified and baselined.

b. Planned testing is consistent with defined incremental approach including regression testing.

c. All test facilities and resources (including test personnel, (lab test stations, hardware, and software) are ready and available to support software testing within the defined schedule.

d.   The software being tested and the entire test environment is configuration controlled as applicable.

e.   All metrics show readiness for testing.

f.   The problem report system is defined and implemented.

g.   The system test baseline is established and controlled.

h.   CS&S risks (including those related to cost, schedule, and performance) have been identified and mitigation plans have been developed.

F.9   Software Functional Configuration Audit (FCA)

Software FCAs should be conducted for each CSCI in the system. Software audits may be conducted on a single CSCI or a group of CSCIs. This audit is intended to confirm the CSCI is verified/tested relative to the allocated requirements in the SRS, IRSs, and relevant higher level specifications. Software FCAs also verify tested CSCIs were designed, coded, and tested following defined processes identified to be applied on the program in the IMP and supporting plans to include the software development plan, the configuration management plan, and the test plans.

Software FCAs may be performed incrementally on increments of software (i.e. planned partial functional capability increments, sometimes called blocks). In such cases, a final software FCA should be conducted to ensure all specified requirements have been satisfied. In cases where CSCI verification can only be completely determined after system integration and testing, the final FCA should be conducted using the results of these tests.

F.9.1   Inputs/Entry Criteria

a.   System and subsystem functional/development specifications.

b.   CSCI functional/development specifications, e.g., SRS and IRS.

c.   Draft CSCI product design specifications.

d.   Unresolved software related test deficiency reports.

e.   Software test plans, descriptions, and procedures.

F.9.2   Outputs (Exit Criteria)

a.   CSCI allocated baselines for software functions.

b.   Verification of CSCI functional/performance requirements (i.e., verification/test results sufficient to establish specified functional/performance requirements have been satisfied).

c.   Readiness for next level of FCA.

d.   Software FCA minutes identifying open discrepancies and actions for resolution.

e.   Relevant software metrics.

f.   Determination that the CSCI is fit for intended use (i.e., remaining discrepancies or any requirements not passed do not prevent the software from safe use in the intended environment).

F.10   CS&S Support to the System Functional Configuration Audit (FCA)

Functional Configuration Audits (FCAs) are conducted to verify CI/CSCIs have achieved the requirements in their functional/performance requirements' specifications. The specific tasks addressed here are the FCA activities necessary to confirm adequacy and completeness of the verification of the computer hardware CIs, and software CSCIs. For CSCIs, the audit verifies that the specified requirements are satisfied as demonstrated and recorded in the verification records (test results).

A series of FCAs is normally held to cover each relevant CI/CSCI in a new development, and they can also be held in the Production and Deployment phase for modifications, upgrades and product improvements. The entry and exit accomplishments for this review are to be included in the IMP. FCAs are an incremental part of the SVR activity.

An FCA may be conducted in increments. In such cases, a final FCA should be conducted to ensure that all requirements of the FCA have been satisfied. In cases where item verification can only be completely determined after system integration and testing, the (final) FCA should be conducted using the results of these tests.

F.10.1   Inputs/Entry Criteria
a. System and subsystem functional/development specifications.
b. CI and CSCI functional/development specifications, e.g., SRS and IRS.
c. Draft CI and CSCI product design specifications.
d. Unresolved CS&S related test deficiency reports.
e. CS&S test plans, descriptions, and procedures.

F.10.2   Outputs (Exit Criteria)
a. CI and CSCI allocated baselines for CS&S functions.
b. Verification of CI and CSCI functional/performance requirements, i.e., verification/test results sufficient to establish specified functional/performance requirements have been satisfied.
c. Readiness for next level of FCA or readiness for production.
d. FCA minutes identifying open discrepancies and actions for resolution.

F.11   CS&S Support to the System Verification Review (SVR)

The System Verification Review (SVR) is a multi-disciplined product and process assessment to ensure that the system under review can proceed into Low-Rate Initial Production and Full-Rate Production within cost (program budget), schedule (program schedule), risk, and other system constraints. Generally this review is an audit trail from the Critical Design Review. It assesses the system final product, as evidenced in its production configuration, and determines if it meets the functional requirements (derived from the Capability Development Document and draft Capability Production Document) documented in the Functional, Allocated, and Product Baselines. The SVR establishes and verifies final product performance. It provides inputs to the Capability Production Document. The SVR is often conducted concurrently with the Production

Readiness Review. A Functional Configuration Audit may also be conducted concurrently with the SVR, if desired. [From the Defense Acquisition Guidebook.]

Configuration items (CIs), subsystems and the system are verified to satisfy the performance and functional requirements contained in the functional and allocated baselines. The completeness of the CS&S verifications are confirmed as integrated with the total system. SVR is the culmination of incremental reviews which confirms completeness of the products (i.e. CIs, CSCIs, and the subsystems which comprise the system). The FCA part of the SVR audits the adequacy and compliance with the verification process, as well as the completeness and sufficiency of the recorded verification/test results relative to the specified requirements.

For the CS&S CIs, CSCIs, and subsystems, verification testing should be accomplished prior to the system SVR as planned events in the IMP and the supporting SDP. This verification process should include, for example, FCAs for each CSCI. Traceability among system through CSCI requirements, design, and code should be verified.

F.11.1   Inputs/Entry Criteria

    a. Completed incremental FCAs for each CS&S CI, CSCI and subsystem.

    b. System and subsystem functional/development specifications.

    c. CI and CSCI functional/development specifications, e.g., SRS and IRS.

    d. CI and CSCI product design specifications.

    e. Verification/test results for each CS&S CI, CSCI, and subsystem confirming compliance with specified requirements, i.e. all section 4 verification requirements against section 3 performance requirements.

F.11.2   Outputs (Exit Criteria)

    a. CI and CSCI allocated baselines for CS&S functions.

    b. Verification of CI and CSCI functional/performance requirements (i.e., verification/test results sufficient to establish specified functional/performance requirements have been satisfied).

    c. CI and CSCI product specifications are baselined.

    d. Software requirements, design and code traceability are established.

    e. Software CSCIs are verified through hardware/software and subsystem integration and test.

    f. Software implementation is verified against specified system requirements.

    g. Readiness for production.

    h. FCA minutes identifying open discrepancies and actions for resolution.

    i. Required operational and support manuals/documents/electronic data bases, to include software development files, are complete and available.

F.12   Software Physical Configuration Audit (PCA)

Software Physical Configuration Audits (PCAs) may be held for individual CSCIs or aggregations of CSCIs. The results of these software PCAs would become entrance criteria to the system PCA. For CSCIs the PCA is usually held at the end of the SD&D phase, but it should not be started unless the FCA for that CSCI has been completed or is being accomplished concurrently. The entry and exit accomplishments for the PCA should be included in the IMP.

For CSCIs, the PCA includes a detailed audit of design documentation, listings, and operation and support documents. The documentation to be audited typically includes the SPS, Interface Design Document (IDD), and Version Description Document (VDD), or their equivalents. The software PCA should include an audit of the released quality control records to make sure the as-coded configuration item is reflected by this documentation. Satisfactory completion of software PCA and approval of the product specification and interface design document, or their equivalents, are necessary to establish the CSCI's Product Baseline.

For the software PCA, the contractor should identify any differences between the physical configuration of the CSCI and the configuration that was used for the software FCA. A list delineating both approved and outstanding changes against the CSCI should be provided and it should identify approved specification change notices (SCNs) and approved deviations/waivers to the software and interface requirements specifications.

F.12.1   Inputs/Entry Criteria

a. Software requirements specifications, including interface requirements specifications.

b. CSCI product specifications, including interface specifications.

c. Software computer program source code listings.

d. Satisfactory completion of the system, subsystem and CI/CSCI SVRs and FCAs including test reports showing that all tests have been performed as required.

e. Satisfactory completion of the software FCAs.

f. Whether electronic or paper documentation, the information defining the exact design of the CSCI is identified, internally controlled, and ready for software PCA.

g. All required software information, whether electronic or documentation, has been confirmed ready for audit.

F.12.2   Outputs (Exit Criteria)

a. Software PCA discrepancies have been documented as action items with specific action organizations and suspense dates established for resolution of the discrepancies.

b. Software product CSCI specifications have been verified against the as-coded software.

c. Software support and operational information is completed and verified for accuracy.

d. Version description documents are completed and verified for accuracy.

F.13   CS&S Support to the System Physical Configuration Audit (PCA)

Physical Configuration Audits (PCAs) are a formal examination of an "as-built" configuration item against its technical documentation to establish or verify the configuration item's product baseline. A PCA should be held for each CI after completion of the acceptance testing (and SVR/FCA) of

----

the first system designated for operational deployment. This review should be conducted in accordance with established configuration management guidelines.

A system PCA is conducted to confirm all CI/CSCI PCAs have been satisfactorily completed; items that can be baselined only at the system-level have been baselined; and required changes to previously completed baselines have been implemented (e.g., deficiencies discovered during testing have been resolved and implemented).

For CSCIs, the PCA is usually held at the end of the SD&D phase, but should not be started unless the FCA for that CSCI has been completed or is being accomplished concurrently. The entry and exit accomplishments for the PCA should be included in the IMP.

For CSCIs, the PCA includes a detailed audit of design documentation, listings, and operation and support documents. The documentation to be audited includes the SPS, IDD, and VDD, or their equivalents. The PCA should include an audit of the released quality control records to make sure the as-coded configuration item is reflected by this documentation. Satisfactory completion of a PCA and approval of the product specification and interface design document, or their equivalents, are necessary to establish the CSCI's product baseline.

For the PCA, the contractor should identify any difference between the physical configuration of the CSCI and the configuration that was used for the FCA. A list delineating both approved and outstanding changes against the CSCI should be provided and should identify approved SCNs and approved deviations/waivers to the software and interface requirements' specifications.

F.13.1   Inputs/Entry Criteria

    a. Satisfactory completion of the relevant CI/CSCI PCAs.

    b. System, subsystem, and CI/CSCI product specifications, including interface specifications.

    c. Satisfactory completion of the system, subsystem and CI/CSCI SVRs and FCAs including test reports showing that all tests have been performed as required.

    d. Whether electronic or paper documentation, the information defining the exact design of the CI and CSCI is identified, internally controlled, and ready for PCA.

    e. All required CS&S information, whether electronic or document, has been confirmed ready for audit.

F.13.2   Outputs (Exit Criteria)

    a. CS&S PCA discrepancies have been documented as action items with specific action organizations and suspense dates established for resolution of the discrepancies.

    b. Software product CSCI specifications have been verified against the as-coded software.

    c. Computer systems product CI specifications have been verified against the as-built product.

    d. CS&S support and operational information is completed and verified for accuracy.

    e. Version description documents are completed and verified for accuracy.

    f. Software is ready to transition to sustainment.

Appendix G
Process Considerations for
Safety Critical Systems

G.1   Introduction

This appendix provides an outline for the acquisition and development process steps to be followed when acquiring and developing safety critical systems. It is crucial to avoid limiting the scope of safety processes to software only. The software, hardware, and entire system architecture must be addressed. A fundamental flaw with some existing process standards is the predominant focus on software processes, while ignoring the overall system. As computer system capabilities have matured to highly integrated (functionally and physically) system architectures, it has become imperative to expand the development and acquisition processes to address system attributes. It has for years been standard practice in the safety critical environment to address the entire system as safety critical, by thoroughly evaluating all functional threads throughout the system. As the implementation of safety critical functionality extends to other systems, this system focus must now be applied in areas where it has not been used extensively in the past.

The process steps described in this appendix are integral to the successful design, development, integration, and test of safety critical systems. Process sections focus heavily on safety considerations. Cost, schedule, performance, and support risks are not addressed directly, although they are inherent in the overall process. Following a thorough process as defined here reduces overall life cycle costs, minimizes schedule delays, allows for more rapid system changes, and enhances safety by design.

Note: These processes have been applied successfully to numerous aircraft flight-critical systems, and they have been generalized here. Where there are still flight-systems references, the reader should generalize to his/her specific domain.

G.2   Systems Approach

G.2.1   Architecture Trade Studies

The system architecture provides the fundamental mechanization of the system. An insufficient architecture will restrict system performance, processing capability, system flexibility, functional integration capability, and supportability; and will limit the computing system's ability to satisfy safety requirements. Understanding and defining the capability of the architecture early will minimize development and support issues; will help contain technical, cost, and schedule risks; and will reduce architecture technical/safety risks.

Trade study analysis should identify the technical feasibility of candidate architectures. Architectural trade studies should evaluate:

    a.   Developer's experience integrating similar architectures.

    b.   Performance requirements of the computational system.

    c.   Architectural element maturity, compatibility, and viability.

    d.   Capability and availability of candidate hardware.

    e.   Functional interlacing throughout the computer system architecture.

    f.   Safety and security requirements.

    g.   Safety risks.

        (1)   Weaknesses in architecture mechanization.

        (2)   Mitigation strategies.

    h.   Technical complexity.

    i.   Software sizing.

    j.   Required interface types.

    k.   Data rates and bandwidth sizing to support system level requirements.

    l.   Supportability of system.

    m. Cost and schedule constraints of candidate architecture.

    n.   Perform an analysis that forecasts future requirements and functional capabilities that could eventually be levied upon the system.

Early in the system design, consideration should be given to the functional and physical separation of safety critical systems and subsystems from non-safety critical systems and subsystems. Functional separation usually leads to the physical separation of safety critical systems from mission critical systems.

G.2.2 Architecture System Requirements Review (SRR)

A review of the architecture as part of the SRR shall be conducted to evaluate the adequacy of the overall architecture. The architecture should be assessed to ensure that critical elements are implemented to achieve a safe design. The review shall evaluate all design attributes such as redundancy, redundancy management, fault tolerant characteristics, and safety risk mitigation techniques employed to perform SCFs and computer system requirements. When components having different safety criticalities are mixed on the same computing platform, then all components must be developed to the highest safety criticality level.

A successful SRR addressing the architecture should address the following:

    a.   Definition of system requirements.

    b.   Definition of safety requirements.

    c.   Definition of architecture performance requirements, incorporating worst case loading and sizing requirements, then allowing extra size for future modifications.

    d.   Definition of requirements flow to lower levels.

    e.   Definition of interface between requirements interface definition.

    f.   Allocation of criticality to requirements.

    g.   Identification of supportability requirements.

h.   Evaluation of architecture trade study results.

i.   Identification of key architecture design attributes.

j.   Determination of technological challenges of the architecture selected.

k.   Determination of testability of candidate architecture.

l.   Investigation of risk mitigation techniques employed throughout the architecture.

m.   Determination of how the architecture supports SCF's.

G.2.3   Safety Critical Function (SCF) Thread Analysis

Identifying the SCF threads through the architectural design is imperative in order to understand how criticality affects components and the entire architecture. Once these effects are understood, proper architecture risk mitigation strategies may be developed and employed.

A SCF thread analysis shall be performed to identify the flow of SCFs through the architectural design. The thread analysis shall be reviewed at the SRR and all subsequent design reviews as the design matures. The analysis shall identify all safety critical functions performed by the weapon system. Each hardware or software component that supports a SCF(s) shall have a safety criticality classification at a level equivalent to the function it supports and shall be developed according to its classification level. Hardware/software components that support functions of multiple safety criticalities shall be developed at the highest level criticality supported.

When performing SCF Thread Analysis it is crucial to establish well defined safety definitions. Safety definitions should be defined for each level of process definition that the program wants to apply to the development. Examples of safety definitions include safety critical, safety significant, flight critical, and mission critical. Fail-operational and fail-safe system safety requirements, which directly affect the architectural design mechanization, must be defined up-front so that during the SCF Thread Analysis the architecture can be evaluated to ensure requirements are satisfactorily met. In order to effectively perform a SCF Thread Analysis:

a.   Separate the weapon system into its individual segments and identify all of the safety critical functions for the weapon system.

b.   Trace each safety critical function through the various systems that comprise the segments of the weapon system.

c.   Separate each system into its various sub-systems and trace the safety critical function through these sub-systems.

d.   Separate each sub-system into its hardware and software configuration items and trace the safety critical function(s) through these components.

e.   Separate each CSCI into its CSCs and CSUs, and trace the safety critical function through these elements. Examine the safety critical function trace. All hardware/software that supports/processes safety critical functions should also be treated as safety critical.

f.   Analyze the architecture, evaluating levels of redundancy, single point failures, weaknesses in thread coverage, effect on architecture trade study results, redundancy management scheme, and relative level of fault tolerance required for each functional thread.

G.2.4   System Requirements Allocation and Traceability

A formal requirements allocation methodology is necessary to capture how higher level requirements are allocated to lower level systems/subsystems/components. To capture and maintain this allocation information it is essential to utilize a requirements traceability tool. There are numerous commercially available automated tools (such as DOORS, RTM, or Clear Case) that can be tailored to a system's application as desired. Traceability of requirements vertically (from the highest level to the lowest level) and horizontally (by various threads) is essential to ensure full requirements coverage. Traceability also helps to identify areas of the software/hardware impacted by a change, determine the testability of the software/hardware, identify the scope of coverage for all levels of testing, and define coupling of functional threads throughout the software/system mechanization including the identification of requirements that support SCFs.

A formal requirements allocation methodology shall be established and employed that captures all system level requirements and appropriately allocates these requirements to lower levels of the system until all requirements have been fully allocated to the lowest level of requirements definition. The methodology shall also capture all derived requirements that are generated for lower level systems/subsystems/components.

As the design for the weapon system evolves, subsystems will be identified and requirements will be allocated to each of these subsystems. Decomposition of system requirements flowed to subsystems, functions, hardware, interfaces, and software should be identified to specify requirements at each of these levels.

As the architecture is further refined, the subsystems' hardware (i.e. computing platforms, processors, cards, back-planes, memory), along with the software (CSCI(s), partitions, operating system, application software) that will be hosted on each platform, and the interfaces (internal and external buses and discretes) are identified and requirements are flowed to each.

The requirements traceability process shall include the following:

   a. Define methodology and process for requirements allocation.

   b. Select tool(s) for tracing requirements, design components and test cases.

   c. Perform requirements allocation process.

   d. Capture requirements in traceability tool (from system level to low level hardware and software components).

   e. Identify and capture within the traceability tool the requirements, design components and test cases that support SCFs.

   f. Link field data (e.g. requirements, components, functions, test components) in order to identify traceable threads to support various areas of development and maintenance. Examples of traceable threads are requirement threads, functional threads, criticality/hazard threads, test threads, & interface threads.

   g. Utilize tool(s) to analyze identified threads and evaluate/assess adequacy of test coverage.

   h. Establish low level regression testing based upon the components threads through the software.

G.2.5   *Failure Modes Effects Analysis (FMEA)*

Determining the adequacy of the computer system architecture for processing safety critical functions is crucial in the preliminary planning and design phase of development. Doing so helps to mature the software/system design early in its development. FMEA, along with the corresponding FMET (see section G.4.1 below), are proven methods for verifying the robustness of the failure management and redundancy management techniques employed. These activities assist in analyzing the criticality of potential failures and ensuring appropriate mechanisms are in place to preclude loss of safety critical functions due to failures. The terms FMEA and FMET refer to specific forms of failure analysis and insertion testing. It is not necessary for the analysis and testing methods employed to go by these names; however the general processes and procedures embodied by these techniques must be performed to ensure the robustness of the design mechanization to handle failures.

The architecture FMEA process, as a minimum, shall include the following:

a. Conduct of architecture trade studies.

b. Establishment of SCFs.

c. Determination of SCF Threads.

d. Architecture decomposition (hardware/software) to components.

e. Analysis of how candidate architecture/component supports SCF threads.

f. 100% identification of the critical failures through Built-In-Test and software monitors.

g. Analysis of how component failure is handled within the architecture.

h. Analysis of how subsystem failure affects architecture robustness.

i. Analysis of how the architecture supports integrated system processing needs with failure(s) present.

j. Analysis of how the architecture addresses single fail, dual fail, combination unlike single fail, triple fail, and order dependent failures.

G.2.6   *System Architecture Risk Mitigation Requirements*

Safety critical requirements drive the criticality classification of lower level systems and configuration items as they are identified in the evolving design. For aircraft systems, the redundancy levels should be derived from the system level Probability Loss of Control (PLOC) (see Joint Service Specification Guide 2008).

To establish an effective risk mitigation strategy within the architecture:

a. Application of the architecture risk drivers (PLOC, reliability, availability, fail-op/fail-safe requirements, and safety critical function support) shall be incorporated into the architecture design solution.

b. Identification of the techniques for mitigating risk and developing a fault tolerant design scheme for the architecture, hardware, and software shall be defined.

c. Identification of the critical faults (hardware, software, system, and function) and the effect on the system when a fault occurs shall be documented and analyzed.

d. Determine the fault tolerant design mechanization for critical faults and the requirements for other faults.

e. Develop a redundancy management design scheme that addresses level of redundancy, complexity of redundancy management mechanization, voting schemes, Built-In-Test (BIT) monitor structure, rate requirements, Cross Channel Data Links (CCDLs), data latency requirements, transient requirements (maximum allowable), accommodation for loss of critical components, and I/O wrap-around/feedback requirements.

Best practice for safety-critical software is to use a disciplined development process that builds in the highest quality (i.e., the software is free from errors and meets all of its requirements).

G.3   Software/Hardware Approach

G.3.1   Software Development and Design

Adhesion to a robust development process is crucial to instilling integrity into the computing system design. Application of disciplined processes based on accepted standards such as DOD-STD-2167A, MIL-STD-498, or IEEE standard 12207 is recommended. The waterfall life cycle along with top-down design and bottom-up testing is still the best methodology. Develop the process based on criticality of the software/system. Early in the development, determine the specific areas of reuse and the integration required. Evaluate potential areas where autocode will be utilized and the impacts to safety, if any. Ensure the process does not allow patches to the compiled source code. Execution of the software structure should be deterministic and the number of states kept to a minimum. The software application must always complete execution with the minor/major frame if cyclic processing is utilized.

If software partitioning (per ARINC 653) is being utilized, it is imperative to not rely on partitioning as the sole means for mitigating safety risk. Software partitioning does not take the place of redundancy, redundancy management, nor fault tolerant design mechanization techniques. For safety critical systems, partitioning of the hardware and separating safety critical software physically and functionally from the mission/non-safety critical software is the first step. The next step is to address the safety critical function partitioning and ensure the operating system and computer system hardware are treated to the highest criticality level of the application software/CSCI/partition residing on the platform. Do not ignore the system aspects of integration simply because a partitioned design mechanization has been chosen.

For safety critical applications, determine how redundancy, redundancy management, and fault tolerance to the fail-operational/fail-safe requirements are accounted for across the entire computing system architecture. Determine the limitations (e.g. processing, throughput loading, memory, I/O loading, buses, build tools utilized, data latencies, system transients, criticality based on SCF thread implementation, weak links of the design, past experience with safety critical systems) of the platform, architecture, operating system, and each application software partition. Thoroughly test the design, hardware, partitioning mechanization, system, and interfaces.

In order to mitigate risks associated with the contractor selection, it is best to select a contractor who has previous experience in safety critical applications and a proven track record. The identification of staffing/skill requirements for the entire process will help to mitigate staffing problems later in the development process. Selecting a programming language with which the developer has significant experience will minimize program technical problems attributed to the learning curve. Minimizing the size and complexity of the software ensures ease of supportability, testability, and helps mitigate the associated risk. The use of automation and auto coding is encouraged to the maximum extent practical, however, auto coding generators must be evaluated to ensure safe, secure, readable, and real-time capable code is generated. Establishing solid software design architectures will enhance system performance, increase system fault tolerance, and ensure risk is mitigated the maximum extent practicable.

The use of a high order computer programming language is required. Ten percent or less of assembly language code is acceptable for machine dependent functions. Any reused software to be used in a safety critical CSCI must be assessed as to whether it was developed and maintained as safety critical, and if it has, then integrated and tested within the new system. An assessment must be conducted as to the maintainability of the software. Software structure, including CSCIs, CSCs, and CSUs must be determined. Standardizing across the computer system platform architecture will minimize the proliferation of support facility tools required.

The Software Engineering Environment (SEE) provides a set of tools which support software development throughout the system lifecycle. The SEE shall be compatible with the selected architecture, hardware, and software. To encourage supportability, the SEE shall be standardized across the entire system. The following shall be considered when establishing a SEE:

a.   Determination of required software development, integration, test and support tools.

b.   Assurance that the SEE will have the capacity to support required testing at all levels and release versions to support program schedules.

G.3.2   *Software Build/Software Loading Requirements*

The combining of multiple CSCIs into a single load image will require the establishment of a process approach for building the image and loading it into the operational system. The following are common software loading constraints, requirements, and best practices:

a.   The overall process for building a load image shall be treated as a system development (design, develop, integrate, and test) process.

b.   The process shall include specific elements to address structure/architecture, common CSCI constraints (e.g. sizing and associated load image requirements) and interfaces, and VDD requirements for each CSCI and load image release.

c.   The process shall address the following for the actual loading of software into the system: time required, equipment required, safety requirements, configuration control requirements, and security requirements.

d.   The software build/release process shall be tested thoroughly, including FMET and the use of prototype builds.

G.3.3   *Digital Hardware Selection*

The selection of the hardware is one of the key foundations for establishing a computing platform which meets program safety, reliability, supportability, maintainability, processing demands, and fault tolerance requirements.

Mature hardware should be utilized, with previous use in safety critical applications preferred. It is advisable not to push state-of-the-art hardware on safety critical systems. Identification of architecture processing requirements to achieve sufficient rates with adequate throughput margin is essential for target hardware. Throughput estimates must be based upon actual timing measurements (in milliseconds). Processor loading must not exceed 90 percent utilization under worst case processing conditions. Processor selection must match rates required for associated memory devices, backplanes, Programmable Logic Array (PLA) devices, CCDLs. Potential impact/plans for hardware growth capability for future modifications, and Diminishing Manufacturing Sources (DMS) issues must be accounted for with hardware selected.

The hardware selection must account for the associated contribution to safety, addressing the reliability of components through FMECA, environmental stress screening, the associated hazardous risks to functions/subsystems/systems due to failure of components though FMEA, and, if failure occurs, the resultant accommodation for single point failure design weaknesses.

G.3.4   *Functional Integration*

Functional Integration is the result of integrating lower level functions and the subsystems that perform them in order to achieve higher level functionality. The higher level functionality depends on the successful operation of the lower level functions. As an example, a fly-by wire vehicle control function is integrated with flight controls, electrical power, hydraulic power, and structural subsystems since it cannot perform successfully without them. Physical elements of functional integration involve communication paths, electrical interfaces, hardware interfaces, data transfer, and the integration of subsystem software sub-functions across subsystems to achieve higher level functionality.

The first step of the process is to identify all functional thread requirements. Then the architecture is analyzed to ensure it has the capability to support functional integration. The processing requirements (e.g. required rates, I/O coupling, sensor feedback, fault tolerant/redundancy management requirements, allowable transients, memory requirements) shall be determined for each functional thread. Integrated function processing requirements shall be determined. All components of the integrated function thread shall be managed to ensure compatibility/availability of the complete integrated function. Any Human in the Loop (HIL) functionality must be designed with the HMI requirements taken into consideration.

G.3.5   *Software Block/Build Implementation*

If a block (major capability release) or build (smaller increments within blocks) software development approach is selected, the contractor shall plan the development to ensure that:

a.   The approach to block or incremental "build" software development is consistent with the partitioning of the total software system.

b.   Schedule durations and phasing allow sufficient time for the block approach, and that multiple releases (builds) are planned for each block.

c.   Staffing will be available to perform the level of parallel development required by the plan.

d.   Development, test, and integration facilities will be available to perform the level of parallel activities required by the plan.

e.   Adequate completion criteria and full/regression testing are established for each block/build of software planned.

f.   Each planned block/build of software has verifiable requirements (controlled specification subsets) that indicate the level of performance expected of the block/build.

g.   Schedule events (milestones and inchstones) are established and incorporated into the systems engineering master schedule.

h.   Software configuration management planning addresses baseline control of parallel efforts.

G.3.6   *Integrated Scheduling*

Developing and managing all the software development activities coupled to the hardware availability and functional needs is imperative for highly integrated systems. Establish an integrated schedule to track key program events, system program events, key components of the system, software version release requirements/dates, block update events, major integrated functional capability releases, all planned testing events (e.g. at all levels: CSU, CSC, CSCI, and integrated systems), planned laboratory build-up, delivery dates (for hardware, software versions, models and development/test assets), and development approach (e.g. waterfall, serial, incremental). If a program has multiple independent concurrent contractual activities, all design, development, integration, and test activities should be considered in the integrated scheduling process. Establish a block integration manager for each block to ensure every aspect is managed appropriately.

G.4   Systems Testing

Note that attention to test and integration laboratories, test approaches, and tools should begin at contract award. For complex, highly integrated, safety critical systems, the comprehensive integration and verification processes required take considerable time to plan and implement. This requires up-front resources (staff, budget, and schedule). In addition, for incremental/ evolutionary development efforts, the integration and verification capabilities must be ready to support the earliest planned deliveries of system capability.

G.4.1   Failure Modes and Effects Testing (FMET)

Extensive testing is imperative for safety critical systems. No commercially available tool or process will eliminate this requirement. As part of the overall test strategy to verify and validate the robustness of the fault tolerance, failure management, and redundancy management design, it is crucial to conduct FMET. Results from FMEA, problems in the problem reporting system, and lessons learned from past experience with a similar design all form the basis for FMET test cases. Determine the effects of failures in software, hardware, systems, functions, component, subsystem, and the entire integrated computer system. Ensure the analysis and testing addresses single point failures, dual failure cases, triple failure cases, combination of single point unlike failures, order dependent failures, loss of function, loss of component, loss of subsystem, loss of redundancy, loss of sensor, loss of feedback, loss of communication/CCDL, loss or degradation of power, and system transient response, regardless of probability. Ensure the analysis and testing addresses SCF threads, hardware/software risk mitigation areas, and all levels of the computer system architecture. Verify that the result of failure correlates to the expected system response. Determine a method for analyzing/fixing identified problems.

FMET testing, done properly, is very comprehensive, and programs should expect to see thousands of test cases identified. It is important to start testing as soon as the design can support testing to mature the design, BIT monitors, fault tolerance, and redundancy management mechanizations.

G.4.2   Hardware Test Process

Thorough testing of the hardware is crucial to the integrity of the computational system performance. It is imperative to ensure the hardware testing addresses the following: processor, memory, circuit boards, Field Programmable Gate Arrays (FPGA), back-plane, design life testing, environmental qualification testing (e.g. sand, dust, shake, bake, and humidity), electromagnetic interference (EMI) testing, hardware interfaces, and processor throughput tests. It is imperative to perform as much testing as early as possible to enable re-procurement for new hardware if test results are unacceptable. Ensure testability is designed into the hardware. Allow for test points external of the circuit cards, boxes, and racks if technically feasible. If unique test software (sometimes referred to as orange software) is utilized in the application software, ensure that it is fully integrated and tested as part of the system. Do not mask hardware problems with software, but if this approach is used, ensure it is well documented and tracked.

G.4.3   Software Test Process

Thorough software testing is the foundation for complete test coverage. With the advent of many software development tools for high order languages and requirements traceability, the capability for automating and structuring the test cases has evolved. Automating software testing facilitates repeatability of testing and expedites testing with each version release. Starting at the lowest level (CSUs) of the software structure, it is imperative to perform path, software construct, failure insertion, signal tolerance, and function testing, as well as peer reviews. The next level (CSCs) is the functional integration of the lowest level (CSUs) of the software which form a function performed by the software. Testing includes stand alone CSCs, function performance, signal tolerance/path, and failure insertion, as well as peer reviews. Many of the CSUs/CSCs are functionally coupled throughout the software (CSC integration) and constitute numerous functional threads, including SCF threads.

Safety interlocks are a design mechanization to enable or disable systems, subsystems, and functions at given times under certain mode conditions. Interlocks are often used to satisfy safety requirements for a system. An interlock should be designed to achieve system performance requirements, some of which may be for safety. As a result, each interlock must be fully analyzed and tested within the context of the system, subsystem, and software design mechanization to ensure a safe implementation. In modern, highly integrated systems, an interlock design can become very complex and may be integrated with other sub-system interlock mechanisms. It is vitally important to ensure that these interlock mechanisms are fully understood, documented, and tested to verify the design is safely integrated.

Each thread must be tested as an entity, including functional thread tests, CSC integration, thread flow execution, and thread/CSC failure insertion tests. Thread testing should also be peer reviewed.

The formal qualification process for software involves a series of formal tests performed on the software loaded onto the target hardware to verify performance of all software level requirements. For safety-critical systems, this formal qualification shall be performed for every flight release. The qualification process typically includes many of the lower level tests up through the system laboratory testing to ensure test coverage for each version release to the air vehicle.

G.4.4   System Integration Process

Establishment of system integration laboratory(s) that replicate the computer system architecture hardware of the integrated systems must be a program priority from the time of contract award. Establish a process to ensure the planned availability of capabilities is in place when needed for integrated system testing. This includes all hardware, software versions, subsystems, functional capabilities, components, models/simulations, and laboratory assets required. This is an iterative build process to mature the test capability around a structured test process. Develop an integrated system test product flow process to understand and manage the product releases from every level (software, hardware, subsystems). This should account for integration and testing of products that are produced by different development organizations, and should also account for building up capability from the lowest level of software components up through subsystems, systems, and segments.

G.4.5   System Test Process

System level testing is imperative in mitigating safety risks and minimizing expensive flight test time for identifying problems with the software, hardware, and systems. With highly integrated computer system architectures, it is necessary to perform extensive testing of the software functionality at the system level. Performing test coverage analysis addressing all areas/levels (functional threads, architecture, hardware, software and system) to determine the areas which must be addressed by the system level facility(s) is an essential first step. It is imperative to couple this process to the system integration process, system architecture risk mitigation process, integrated scheduling process, laboratory architecture development process, laboratory fidelity process, and the FMET process. Generate test plans, procedures, and test cases for all systems/laboratories. In each lab facility, test the system from multiple perspectives; internal to system, internal to functional thread, external to the system, how the system affects other systems/subsystems/functions, and how other systems, subsystems, and functions affect the system. To the maximum extent possible, attempt to minimize duplication of testing.

G.4.6   *Laboratory Architecture Plans for System Testing*

Utilizing high fidelity/highly representative laboratory facilities for integrated system testing is a tremendous means of mitigating risks (e.g. flight safety risks and associated cost of testing on the operational system). Establishing the architecture requirements to test integrated systems with a high degree of fidelity requires careful planning. The entire overarching system integration and testing coverage across one or more complex labs must be evaluated to achieve sufficient test coverage while minimizing test duplication. Planning for representative computer system hardware for dedicated use in the lab facilities is imperative. Labs must replicate the completed system architecture to the maximum extent practicable.

Recognize that some functional threads cannot be tested in a laboratory, and must be tested on the operational system. Plan for the labs to be in existence for the life of the program. They are critical to the operation and sustainment of the system once initial development has been completed. Plan for a lab/test facility manager to manage and control all testing performed in the facility. Labs should be capable of operating at least in a surge mode for 24/7 operation.

G.4.7   *Laboratory Fidelity Process*

Before testing can take place the Laboratory Fidelity Process must be completed in order to determine the adequacy of the laboratories in which testing will occur. The developer shall determine delivery requirements for hardware and test assets and laboratory fidelity requirements (e.g. actual hardware, what will be simulated/emulated/modeled, development tools, test equipment, unique tools (software/hardware/interfaces) which must be developed).

G.4.8   *Regression Test Plans*

Planning for regression testing assumes that the full set of testing has been defined for all levels of testing up through laboratory system integration testing. Typically, for regression testing of safety critical systems in major block updates, the entire suite of tests is performed at all levels. For incremental releases of functionality regression testing is performed. The regression test suite varies depending upon the level of test. For safety critical systems, the CSUs (modified or affected by the modification), CSCs (CSU has changed within CSC), and CSCI formal qualification test (FQT) is completely rerun for every release. This is where the payback comes from automating test cases to the maximum extent possible, in order to expedite regression testing performance. At the system level, a core set of test cases (typically 10 – 40% of the entire test suite) are identified to be run independent of the area of change. Specific test cases are added relative to the functional area of change. If the change is too substantial or complex, it may be necessary to rerun the entire test suite. Regression testing must take into account internal system changes, interfacing software, integrated function elements, hardware changes, sensor and effector changes, rate changes, and component changes. The regression test plan should be well defined prior to delivery of the first operational capability.

G.4.9   *Software/Hardware Change Process*

Changes to the software and hardware are inevitable throughout the life cycle to fix discrepancy reports and improve system testing and maturity. As these changes occur it is imperative that a process is documented for incorporating necessary changes for hardware and software into the computer system architecture with minimal impact to the safe operation. A flow chart shall be developed to document the development process steps to be followed for all potential areas of change, and this process shall tie to established development, test, and regression test processes.

Software in many cases is changed to mask a resultant output or hardware problem instead of actually fixing the true problem. In many hardware related cases, a software fix is the most economical and time effective means of correcting the deficiency, but this must be thoroughly analyzed to ensure a safe solution. The effect that the software change has to safety critical function threads must also be identified and analyzed. Plan to analyze the change for impact to rate changes, system transients, mechanization flow, hardware and interface compatibility, software modules, and other associated effects.

As with the hardware selection process, the hardware change process should utilize mature, reliable components. It is not recommended that state-of-the-art design be pushed. Performance requirements for the system must not be compromised. Once developed, the changed hardware shall be treated as a new development, and as such, fully re-qualified at the system, platform, and software (operating system and application software) levels. The impact of DMS must also be considered when re-developing the hardware. The process shall also determine the regression testing process for the areas changed.

G.5   System Certification Approach

System certification is the process, regardless of domain, that certifies that an acceptable approach has been used in the development and verification of a system, and that the system is acceptable for its intended use. For example, in the case of aircraft, the airworthiness certification process results in clearance to fly, sometimes with restrictions or limitations. Whatever the domain, certification is a capstone process that results in approval authority for installation and operation of new capability and changes affecting operational systems.

G.5.1   System Airworthiness Certification (AWC) Process

For aircraft systems, Airworthiness Certification is well defined in the evaluation criteria contained in MIL-HDBK-516A and B. The completed AWC process ties to the regression test, block/build manager, software loading, and problem reporting processes. The key to passing Airworthiness Certification for safety critical computer systems is to follow thorough development, integration, and test processes without cutting any corners. Following thorough processes will ensure safety is inherently designed into the computer system architecture, mitigating risk and resulting in a robust system design. Section 15 of MIL-HDBK-516 covers all criteria applicable for any safety or flight critical software, hardware, computer architectures, and system integration for air vehicle computer systems.

G.6   Discrepancy Reporting

A process must be established for tracking software, hardware, system, integration, test case, and facility problems in order to document, control, and test the changes required for problems found. Problems should be documented in a discrepancy reporting system at the time of discovery, rather than waiting until the problem is fully analyzed and the source understood. Establish a board to review and disposition corrective action(s) required. Tie the problems reported to the software/hardware change process. Problems should be prioritized based on safety criticality (severity), for example:

   a.   Severity 1: Safety impact (must fix prior to software use in the actual system).

b. Severity 2: Safety impact with known limitation documented in the system operator manual (in general, must fix prior to software use in the actual system).

c. Severity 3: No safety impact, probable operational impact (must be fixed in next planned release or before operational need).

d. Severity 4: No safety impact, no operational impact (could be lab problem).

e. Severity 5: No safety impact, nuisance problem.

Appendix H
Air Force Core Software Metrics

The Air Force program office and development contractors should mutually agree on and implement selected software metrics to provide management visibility into the software development process. The metrics should clearly portray variances between planned and actual performance, should provide early detection or prediction of situations that require management attention, and should support the assessment of the impact of proposed changes on the program. The following core metrics are required:

    a. Software size.

    b. Software development effort.

    c. Software development schedule.

    d. Software defects.

    e. Software requirements definition and stability.

    f. Software development staffing.

    g. Software progress (design, coding, and testing).

    h. Computer resources utilization.

These indicators should be tailored and implemented consistent with the developer's internal tools and processes. Program managers and developers should agree upon and establish additional metrics or means of insight to address software issues deemed critical or unique to the program. All software metrics information should be available to the program manager, ideally through on-line, electronic means. Definitions should be provided to explain metrics such as software size, development effort, and development schedule. Additional information is provided below for each required metric.

H.1   Software Size

The size of the software to be developed/integrated is the most critical factor in estimating the software development effort and schedule. Software size should be estimated and recorded prior to the start of the program and tracked until the completion of development by all programs involving software development or sustainment. Software size should be estimated and tracked at least to the function or CSCI level for each increment or block. It should be re-evaluated at major program milestones or whenever requirements are changed. The actual size should be recorded at the time a capability (increment or block) is delivered. The reasons for changes in software size should also be captured over the development period.

Software size is typically measured in SLOC. For weapon system software development, SLOC is likely the most readily available and the best understood measure. Size should be tracked for new, modified, and reused code. For programs where relatively small changes are being applied to large existing software products, or for development efforts that primarily involve the integration of existing software products, some type of "equivalent lines of code" or some other measure may be appropriate to identify and track the volume of effort required. Whatever measure is used must be clearly defined such that it is easily understandable and can be consistently applied.

Changes in software size may indicate an unrealistic original estimate; instability in requirements, design, or coding; or lack of understanding of requirements. Any of these situations can lead to increases in the cost and schedule required to complete the software. Variations in software size when tracked by increment or block, may indicate migration of capability from earlier to later increments. Software size data collected over time will provide a historical basis for improved software estimating processes.

H.2   Software Development Effort

Software development effort is measured in staff hours or staff months, and directly relates to software development cost. Estimated software development effort is derived primarily from software size, but also depends on other factors such as developer team capability, tool capability, requirements stability, complexity, and required reliability.

When combined with earned value data and other management information, variances in planned and actual effort expended may indicate potential overruns, lack of adequate staff or the proper mix of skills, underestimated software size, unstable or misunderstood requirements, failure to achieve planned reuse, or unplanned rework as a result of software defects.

H.3   Software Development Schedule

Software schedules should be planned to at least the function or CSCI level for each increment or block, and should be re-evaluated at major program milestones or whenever requirements are changed. Planned and actual schedules should be tracked continuously from the start through the completion of development. Software schedules should provide insight into the start and completion dates as well as progress on detailed activities associated with requirements, design, coding, integration, testing, and delivery of software products.

Software development schedule durations are measured in months. Like effort, estimated software development schedules are determined primarily from software size, but also depend on other factors such as developer team capability, tool capability, requirements stability, complexity, required reliability, and software testing methods and tools.

Late or poor quality deliveries of low level software products are indicators of overall program schedule risk. Schedules should be examined for excessive parallel activities that are not realistic when available resources such as staff or integration labs are considered, excessive overlap of activities where dependencies exist, or inconsistent detail or duration for similar tasks.

H.4   Software Defects

Software defects should be tracked by individual software products as part of the system defect tracking process from the time the products are initially baselined. Software defects should be tracked at the function or CSCI level or lower, by increment or block.

Defects are measured by tracking problem reports. Problem reports should account for missing or poorly defined requirements that result in software rework or unplanned effort. Problem reports may be tracked by category or criticality, including total number of problem reports written, open, and closed. These could be further broken down by additional categories, including development phase (requirements definition and analysis, design, code, developer test, and system test) in which the problem was inserted, development phase in which the problem was discovered, or by severity.

Software defect metrics provide insight into the readiness of the software to proceed to the next phase, its fitness for intended use, and the likelihood/level of future rework. Analysis of software defects may also indicate weaknesses in parts of the development process, or may identify certain software components that are particularly troublesome and thus contribute greater program risk.

H.5   *Software Requirements Definition and Stability*

The number of software requirements should be tracked by increment or block over time. The number of changes to software requirements (additions, deletions, or modifications) should be tracked in the same manner. The reasons for requirements changes (new capability or improved understanding derived during development) should also be tracked.

The number of requirements relates to software size and provides an indicator of how the requirements are maturing and stabilizing. Software requirements changes can be an early indicator of rework or unplanned additional software development effort.

H.6   *Software Development Staffing*

Software staffing is tracked using two separate measures. The first tracks the status of the developer's actual staffing level versus the planned staffing profile over time. A separate measure tracks developer turnover (unplanned losses of development personnel that must be replaced). Staffing can also be tracked by personnel type, such as management, engineering, qualification/testing, and quality assurance.

It is common for developers to plan for a rapid personnel buildup at the start of a program, and it is also common for programs to have difficulty ramping up their staff at the planned rate. Late arrival of staff indicates planned up-front work is not being completed on schedule, and will likely lead to delays in delivery, reduced functionality, or both. Turnover adversely impacts productivity through the direct loss of developers, replacement staff learning curve, and the impact on existing staff to support replacement staff familiarization.

H.7   *Software Progress (Design, Coding, and Testing)*

Software progress is used to track over time, down to the lowest level of software components, the actual completion of development phase activities compared to the program plan. A typical approach to progress tracking involves measuring the actual number of software components or units designed, coded, or tested compared to the planned rate of completion.

Failure to complete these lower level development activities according to schedule is an indication that there will likely be impact to program-level schedules.

H.8   *Computer Resources Utilization*

Weapon system software often "grows" to fill or exceed the available computing system capacity. Because of that, it is necessary to track computer resources utilization. Computer resources utilization is a measure of the percentage of computing resources consumed by the planned or actual software operating in a worst case but realistic processing load. Engineering analysis is required to define realistic worst case scenarios the system is expected to encounter. Utilization is measured as a percentage of capacity used for processing, memory, input/output, and communication links. This measure should be tracked as an estimate in the early phases of system development, and actuals as the system continues through development/integration.

Monitoring computer resources utilization helps ensure the planned software design and expected capabilities will fit within the planned computer resources, and that adequate reserve capacity is available to permit some level of enhancement in the post deployment support phase. Overloaded computer resources can lead to system instability or other unacceptable performance.

Appendix I
Software Development Plan

The SDP describes a developer's plans for conducting a software development effort. The term "software development" in this context is meant to include new development, modification, reuse, reengineering, maintenance, and all other activities resulting in software products. The SDP provides the acquirer insight into, and a tool for monitoring, the processes to be followed for software development, the methods to be used, approach to be followed for each activity, organization, and resources. The SDP should be developed in the contractor's preferred format, and should document all processes applicable to the system to be acquired, at a level of detail sufficient to allow the use of the SDP as the full guidance for the developers. It should contain or reference specific standards, methods, tools, actions, reuse strategy, and responsibility associated with the development and qualification of all requirements, including safety and security.

The SDP should contain the following information, as applicable:

    a. Plan introduction and overview.

        (1) Purpose, scope, and objectives.

        (2) Assumptions and constraints.

        (1) Relationship to other program plans.

        (2) Referenced documents.

        (3) Identification of all software and software products to which the SDP applies.

        (4) Definition of terms and acronyms.

    b. System overview, including system and software architecture.

    c. Overview of required work, including:

        (1) Requirements and constraints on the system and software to be developed.

        (2) Software products and related deliverables.

        (3) Requirements and constraints on project documentation.

        (4) The program/acquisition strategy, resources, and schedules with respect to any related requirements or constraints.

        (5) Additional requirements and constraints such as on project security, privacy, methods, standards, interdependencies in hardware and software development.

        (6) Known software-specific risks.

    d. Project organization and resources, including:

        (1) Identification of all organizations with software development responsibilities.

        (2) Identification of all software to be developed by organization.

(3)   Identification of personnel resources, including staff loading (number of personnel overtime), breakdown by responsibility (management, software engineering, testing), and specific skills and training.

(4)   Identification and standards for use of tools (such as those used for requirements management, test management, configuration management).

(5)   Identification of required development equipment, facilities, and test/integration laboratories (including requirements analysis and tracking tools, compilers, assemblers, editors, debuggers, configuration management tools, code analyzers, code auditors, simulations, software development libraries and files, software development labs, and test/integration labs).

(6)   Applicable developer (internal) processes, procedures, and work instructions.

e.   Plans for performing general software development activities, including:

(1)   Software development processes.

(2)   Software development methods.

(3)   Software development standards (including coding standards, guidelines, practices, and processes used in the design and development of the software).

(4)   Reusable software products and COTS.

(5)   Software types/categories (i.e., operational software, test software, support equipment software) and associated processes, controls, and documentation.

(6)   Handling of critical requirements (such as safety, security, and information assurance).

(7)   Incremental development approach, planning, and management/oversight.

(8)   Establishing the system/software engineering environment.

(9)   Computer resources utilization and reserve capacity/growth management.

f.   Software-related development processes, including:

(1)   Overall development methodology.

(2)   Prototyping and simulations.

(3)   System requirements analysis and design, including requirements definition and allocation from the system level to the software level.

(4)   Software requirements analysis.

(5)   Software preliminary and detailed design.

(6)   Software unit integration and testing.

(7)   Software component integration and testing.

(8)   CSCI qualification testing.

(9)   CSCI/HWCI integration and testing.

    (10) System qualification testing.

    (11) Determination of fitness for intended use.

    (12) Other developmental testing (such as flight testing).

g. Supporting processes and information, including:

    (1) Software risk management.

    (2) Approach to requirements traceability.

    (3) Software documentation, sufficient to capture and maintain all relevant design information.

    (4) Approach for evaluating, selecting, and integrating COTS and reused software.

    (5) Approach to designing for reuse.

    (6) Open source software approach including a description of the code, its specific origin, how it will be controlled, how it will be tested or analyzed for vulnerabilities, what vulnerabilities have been identified and overcome, and why such code is not a risk to the program.

    (7) Prototyping and simulations.

    (8) Software configuration management, including configuration baselines, audits, problem identification/reporting/tracking/disposition, and patch definition and control.

    (9) Software quality assurance, including software product evaluation.

    (10) Technical reviews, audits (including entry/exit criteria), and other meetings.

    (11) Approach for detailed tracking of all software builds and all related tasks and activities, such as unit code, test, and integration, including allocation of specific software requirements to identified block or builds as well as the process to ensure consistency and integration of software schedules with the program IMP and IMS.

    (12) Status assessment and reporting (EVM, software metrics definition and use, technical performance measures).

    (13) Approach for problem tracking, reporting, and corrective action.

    (14) Approach for managing reserve computing capacity and growth, including margin allocation and budgeting, reserve capacity and growth management and monitoring.

    (15) Approach for conducting information assurance and vulnerability analyses, detection, and prevention techniques throughout the software design and development lifecycle, including for COTS, reused, or modified products.

    (16) Supplier/subcontractor management, including flowdown of processes to suppliers/subcontractors, including the specific relationships of subcontractor SDPs.

    (17) Process improvement activities.

    (18) Support/sustainment approach/processes.

Further information on SDP content is provided in <u>DI-IPSC-81427</u>, and in IEEE/EIA Standard 12207.1, including section 6.5.3a.

Appendix J
Glossary of Supporting Information

J.1   References

FEDERAL

Government Accountability Office (GAO), *Cost Assessment Guide – Best Practices for Estimating and Managing Program Costs (Exposure Draft)*, GAO-07-1134SP, July 2007, http://www.gao.gov/new.items/d071134sp.pdf

National Security Agency, National Information Assurance Partnership, http://www.nsa.gov/ia/industry/niap.cfm

National Security Telecommunications and Information Systems Security Policy (NSTISSP) No. 11, July 2003 http://www.cnss.gov/Assets/pdf/nstissp_11_fs.pdf

Section 804, "Improvement of Software Acquisition Processes," Public Law 107-314, *Bob Stump National Defense Authorization Act for Fiscal Year 2003*, 2 December 2002. http://www.dod.mil/dodgc/olc/docs/PL107-314.pdf

DEPARTMENT OF DEFENSE

Defense Acquisition Guidebook

Defense Acquisition Guidebook on EVM

Defense Acquisition Performance Assessment (DAPA) Report, 2006, http://www.acq.osd.mil/dapaproject/

Defense Acquisition University (DAU), http://www.dau.mil/

Defense Acquisition University Training Center, http://training.dau.mil

Defense Contract Management Agency (DCMA), http://www.dcma.mil/

Defense Cost Resource Center,

———, Cost and Software Data Reporting (CSDR) Contracting Information, http://dcarc.pae.osd.mil/Policy/csdr/csdrContracting.aspx

———, Cost and Software Data Reporting (CSDR) Plan, http://dcarc.pae.osd.mil/Policy/csdr/dd2794.xls

———, Cost and Software Data Reporting (CSDR) Planning Forms and Instructions, http://dcarc.pae.osd.mil/Policy/csdr/csdrForms.aspx

———, Software Resources Data Report, http://dcarc.pae.osd.mil/Policy/srdr/index.aspx?AspxAutoDetectCookieSupport=1

Defense Federal Acquisition Regulation Supplement (DFARS)
> http://www.acq.osd.mil/dpap/dars/index.html
> http://www.acq.osd.mil/dpap/dars/dfarspgi/current/index.html

Defense Technical Information Center (DTIC), http://www.dtic.mil/

Deskbook or Acquisition Knowledge Sharing System (AKSS)

DI-IPSC-81427, Software Development Plan (SDP),
> http://docimages.assistdocs.com/watermarker/transient/65BC89AE6C014F9D9F743C08B0FE18E3.pdf

DI-MGMT-81739, Software Resources Data Reporting: Initial Developer Report and Data Dictionary,
> http://www.assistdocs.com/search/document_details.cfm?ident_number=275661&StartRow=1&PaginatorPageNumber=1&doc%5Fnumber=81739&status%5Fall=ON&search%5Fmethod=BASIC

DI-SAFT-81626, System Safety Program Plan (SSPP),
> http://www.assistdocs.com/search/document_details.cfm?ident_number=212277&StartRow=1&PaginatorPageNumber=1&doc%5Fnumber=81626&status%5Fall=ON&search%5Fmethod=BASIC

DoD AT&L Acquisition Community Connection, Risk Management Community of Practice

DoD Open Technology Development Roadmap, April 2006,
> http://www.acq.osd.mil/jctd/articles/OTDRoadmapFinal.pdf

DoD 5000.04-M-1, *Cost and Software Data Reporting (CSDR) Manual*,
> http://www.dtic.mil/whs/directives/corres/html/500004m1.htm
> http://dcarc.pae.osd.mil/Policy/csdr/500004m1p.pdf

DOD-STD-2167A, *Defense System Software Development*,
> http://assistdocs.com/search/document_details.cfm?ident_number=37303&StartRow=1&PaginatorPageNumber=1&doc%5Fnumber=2167&status%5Fall=ON&search%5Fmethod=BASIC

DoDD 5000.01, *The Defense Acquisition System*,
> http://www.dtic.mil/whs/directives/corres/pdf/500001p.pdf

DoDD 5200.39, *Security, Intelligence, and Counterintelligence Support to Acquisition Program Protection*, http://www.dtic.mil/whs/directives/corres/html/520039.htm

DoDD 8500.1, *Information Assurance (IA)*,
> http://www.dtic.mil/whs/directives/corres/pdf/850001p.pdf

DoDI 8500.2, *Information Assurance (IA) Implementation*,
> http://www.dtic.mil/whs/directives/corres/html/850002.htm

Final Developer Report, http://dcarc.pae.osd.mil/Policy/csdr/DI-MGMT-81739.pdf

Information Assurance Support Environment (IASE), http://iase.disa.mil/

Initial Government Report and Data Dictionary,
> http://dcarc.pae.osd.mil/Policy/csdr/InitialGovernmentReportInstructionsjwbv7.pdf

JSSG-2008, *Vehicle Control and Management System (VCMS)*,
    http://assistdocs.com/search/document_details.cfm?ident_number=205109&StartRow=1&
    PaginatorPageNumber=1&doc%5Fnumber=2008&status%5Fall=ON&search%5Fmethod=
    BASIC, order from Engineering.Standards@wpafb.af.mil

MIL-HDBK-61, *Configuration Management Guidance*,
    http://docimages.assistdocs.com/watermarker/transient/EADE6BE9D3C64BD78796984A9
    809E0CA.pdf

MIL-HDBK-516B, *Airworthiness Certification Criteria*,
    http://www.assistdocs.com/search/document_details.cfm?ident_number=212162&StartRo
    w=1&PaginatorPageNumber=1&doc%5Fnumber=516&status%5Fall=ON&search%5Fmeth
    od=BASIC

MIL-STD-498, *Software Development and Documentation*,
    http://assistdocs.com/search/document_details.cfm?ident_number=114847&StartRow=1&
    PaginatorPageNumber=1&doc%5Fnumber=498&status%5Fall=ON&search%5Fmethod=B
    ASIC

MIL-STD-882, *System Safety*,
    http://docimages.assistdocs.com/watermarker/transient/6E53FECE9FBE44D68450D69759
    9569CA.pdf

OSD Guidance on Earned Value Management (EVM), http://www.acq.osd.mil/pm/

OSD *Systems Engineering Plan (SEP) Preparation Guide*, 18 October 2007, Version 2.0,
    http://www.acq.osd.mil/sse/guidance.html

Risk Management Guide for DoD Acquisition

Scientific and Technical Information Network (STINET), http://stinet.dtic.mil/

Software Program Manager's Network, *The Program Manager's Guide to Software Acquisition
    Best Practices*

AIR FORCE

Aeronautical Systems Center (ASC), *Software Acquisition Engineering Guidebook*

AFI 63-101, *Operations of Capabilities Based Acquisition System*,
    http://www.e-publishing.af.mil/shared/media/epubs/AFI63-101.pdf

AFI 63-1201, *Life Cycle Systems Engineering*, Attachment 8,
    http://www.e-publishing.af.mil/shared/media/epubs/AFI63-1201.pdf

AFMC Pamphlet 63-101, *Risk Management*

Air Force Federal Acquisition Regulation Supplement (AFFARS) Mandatory Procedure 5315.3,
    http://farsite.hill.af.mil/reghtml/regs/far2afmcfars/af_afmc/affars/5315.htm#P41_1691

Air Force Information Assurance (IA) Community of Practice (CoP)

Air Force Institute of Technology (AFIT) Software Professional Development Program (SPDP)
    http://www.afit.edu/ls/spdp_overview.cfm

Air Force Software Technology Support Center (STSC), http://www.stsc.hill.af.mil/
http://www.stsc.hill.af.mil/crosstalk/2006/06/0606Jones.html

————, Guidelines for Successful Acquisition and Management of Software-Intensive Systems,
http://www.stsc.hill.af.mil/resources/tech_docs/gsam4.html

CrossTalk Journal, AF STSC, http://www.stsc.hill.af.mil/crosstalk/

Focus Week Training: *High Confidence Programs*

SAF/AQ & SAF/XC Memo, *Implementation of OTD*, 20 December 2007.

SAF/AQ/US Memorandum 04A-003, *Revitalizing the Software Aspects of Systems Engineering*,
20 September 2004,

Space and Missile Systems Center (SMC), *Software Acquisition Handbook*

OTHER PUBLICATIONS

ARINC 653, *Avionics Application Software Standard Interface*, http://www.arinc.com/

Boehm, Barry W., *Software Engineering Economics*, January 1994

Boehm, Barry W. and Richard E. Fairley, "Software Estimation Perspectives", *IEEE Software*,
Nov-Dec 2000

Brooks, Frederick P., "Essence and Accidents of Software Engineering," *IEEE Computer*, April
1987

Charette, Robert N., *Liar, Fool, or Both?*,
http://www.compaid.com/caiinternet/ezine/charette-liars.pdf

Data Analysis Center for Software (DACS) Gold Practice, *Formal Risk Management*

EIA-649, *National Consensus Standard for Configuration Management*, Government Electronics
and Information Technology Association, 2004, http://www.eia.org/

IEEE/EIA 12207.1, *Industry Implementation of International Standard ISO/IEC 12207*,
http://standards.ieee.org/

ISO/IEC 12207 (IEEE Standard 12207-2008): *Systems and Software Engineering – Software Life
Cycle Processes*, http://standards.ieee.org/

ISO/IEC 16085 (IEEE Standard 16085-2006): *Systems and Software Engineering – Life Cycle
Processes – Risk Management*, http://standards.ieee.org/

Jones, Capers, *Assessment and Control of Software Risks*, Prentice Hall, 1994

————, *How Software Estimation Tools Work*, 27 February 2005,
http://www.compaid.com/caiinternet/ezine/capers-estimation.pdf

————, *Positive and Negative Innovations in Software Engineering*, 2006,
http://www.compaid.com/caiinternet/ezine/capers-POSNEG.pdf

————, *Software Estimating Rules of Thumb*, 20 March 2007,
http://www.compaid.com/caiinternet/ezine/capers-rules.pdf

Open Source Initiative (OSI), http://opensource.org/

Open Source Report 2008, http://scan.coverity.com/report/

Practical Software and Systems Measurement (PSM), http://www.psmsc.com/

Reifer, Donald J., "The Poor Person's Guide to Estimating Software Development Costs," *IEEE ReadyNotes*, 2006

Software Engineering Institute (SEI),

————, Capability Maturity Model Integration (CMMI), http://www.sei.cmu.edu/cmmi/

————, Goal-Driven Software Measurement—A Guidebook,
http://www.sei.cmu.edu/publications/documents/96.reports/96.hb.002.html

————, Phillips, David M., *Choosing a Supplier: Due Diligence and CMMI*, News@SEI, 2004 Number 2, CMMI in Focus, http://www.sei.cmu.edu/news-at-sei/columns/cmmi-in-focus/2004/2/cmmi-in-focus-2004-2.htm

————, Published Appraisal Results Site (PARS), http://sas.sei.cmu.edu/pars/pars.aspx

————, Software Acquisition Planning Guidelines, December 2005,
http://www.sei.cmu.edu/pub/documents/05.reports/pdf/05hb006.pdf

————, Software Engineering Measurement and Analysis (SEMA), http://www.sei.cmu.edu/sema/

————, Understanding and Leveraging a Supplier's CMMI Efforts: A Guidebook for Acquirers,
http://www.sei.cmu.edu/publications/documents/07.reports/07tr004.html

J.2   Acronyms

ACA-------------------- Associate Contractor Agreement
ACAT------------------ Acquisition Category
ACE-------------------- Acquisition Center of Excellence
ADS-------------------- Appraisal Disclosure Statement
AF---------------------- Air Force
AFFARS -------------- Air Force Federal Acquisition Regulation Supplement
AFI --------------------- Air Force Instruction
AFIT ------------------- Air Force Institute of Technology
AFKN------------------ Air Force Knowledge Now
AFMC ---------------- Air Force Materiel Command
AKSS------------------ Acquisition Knowledge Sharing System
ANSI------------------- American National Standards Institute
AQ --------------------- Acquisition
ASC-------------------- Aeronautical Systems Center
ASP-------------------- Acquisition Strategy Panel
ASR-------------------- Alternate System Review
AT---------------------- Anti Tamper
AT&L ------------------ Acquisition Technology & Logistics
ATS/MTS------------- Aircrew Training System and Maintenance Training System
AWC------------------- Airworthiness Certification
BCA-------------------- Business Case Analysis
BCR ------------------- Baseline Change Requests
BCWS----------------- Budgeted Cost of Work Scheduled
BIT --------------------- Built-in-Test
BOE ------------------- Basis of Estimate
C&A-------------------- Certification & Accreditation
C&TD----------------- Concept & Technology Development
CARD ---------------- Cost Analysis Requirements Description
CCDL----------------- Cross Channel Data Links
CDA ------------------- Central Design Activity
CDD ------------------ Capabilities Definition Document or Capabilities Development Document
CDR ------------------- Critical Design Review
CDRL----------------- Contractor Data Requirements List
CERT/CC------------- Computer Emergency Response Team Coordination Center
CI----------------------- Configuration Item
CLIN ------------------ Contract Line Item Number
CM -------------------- Configuration Management
CMM----------------- Capability Maturity Model
CMMI----------------- Capability Maturity Model Integration
CMP ------------------ Configuration Management Plan
CONOPS------------- Concept of Operation
CoP -------------------- Community of Practice
CORBA -------------- Common Object Request Broker Architecture
COTS ---------------- Commercial Off The Shelf
CPAF----------------- Cost Plus Award Fee
CPCI------------------ Computer Program Configuration Item

CPFF ----------------- Cost Plus Fixed Fee
CPI -------------------- Critical Program Information
CPIF ------------------ Cost Plus Incentive Fee
CPR ------------------ Contract Performance Report
CRLCMP ------------ Computer Resources Life Cycle Management Plan
CRWG --------------- Computer Resources Working Group
CS-------------------- Computer Software
CS&S---------------- Computer Systems & Software
CSC ------------------ Computer Software Component
CSCI------------------ Computer Software Configuration Item
CSDM ---------------- Computer Systems Diagnostic Manual
CSDR ---------------- Cost and Software Data Reporting Plan
CSOM---------------- Computer System Operators Manual
CSOW -------------- Contractor Statement of Work
CSU ------------------ Computer Software Units
CT--------------------- Critical Technology
CWBS---------------- Contract Work Breakdown Structure
DACS ---------------- Data Analysis Center for Software
DAPA----------------- Defense Acquisition Performance Assessment
DAU ------------------ Defense Acquisition University
DCMA --------------- Defense Contract Management Agency
DCS ------------------ Direct Commercial Sales
DFARS--------------- Defense Federal Acquisition Regulation Supplement
DMS ------------------ Diminishing Manufacturing Sources
DoD------------------- Department of Defense
DRRA ---------------- Data Rights Requirements Analysis
DT&E----------------- Developmental Test & Evaluation
DTIC------------------ Defense Technical Information Center
EAC------------------- Estimate at Completion
ECP------------------- Engineering Change Proposal
EMA ------------------ Expectation Management Agreement
EMI ------------------- Electromagnetic Interference
EN--------------------- Engineering
ETC------------------- Estimate to Complete
EV--------------------- Earned Value
EVM ------------------ Earned Value Management
FAQ------------------- Frequently Asked Questions
FAR------------------- Federal Acquisition Regulations
FCA------------------- Functional Configuration Audit
FFP ------------------- Firm Fixed-Price
FMEA ---------------- Failure Modes and Effects Analysis
FMECA ------------- Failure Modes, Effects, and Criticality Analysis
FMET----------------- Failure Modes and Effects Testing
FMS ------------------ Foreign Military Sales
FOSS---------------- Free and Open Source Software
FPGA---------------- Field Programmable Gate Arrays
FPI -------------------- Fixed-Price Incentive
FQT------------------- Formal Qualification Test

GAO ------------------- Government Accountability Office
GFE------------------- Government Furnished Equipment
GFI-------------------- Government Furnished Information
GFP------------------- Government Furnished Property
GFS------------------- Government Furnished Software
GIG -------------------- Global Information Grid
GNU GPL ----------- GNU General Public License
GOTS ---------------- Government Off The Shelf
GPR ------------------ Government Purpose Rights
HIL --------------------- Human in the Loop
HMI ------------------- Human Machine Interface
HQ -------------------- Headquarters
HSI--------------------- Human Systems Integration
HWCI---------------- Hardware Critical Item
I/O---------------------- Input/Output
IA ----------------------- Information Assurance
IASE ------------------ Information Assurance Support Environment
IBR-------------------- Integrated Baseline Review
ICD-------------------- Initial Capabilities Document or Interface Control Document
IDD-------------------- Interface Design Document
IMP ------------------- Integrated Master Plan
IMS -------------------- Integrated Master Schedule
IP ----------------------- Intellectual Property
IPS -------------------- Integrated Program Summary
IPT -------------------- Integrated Product Team
IR&D------------------ Independent Research & Development
IRA-------------------- Integrated Risk Assessment
IRS--------------------- Interface Requirements Specification
ISO-------------------- International Standards Organization
KPP------------------- Key Performance Parameter
LCMP ---------------- Life Cycle Management Plan
LR----------------------- Limited Rights
LRU-------------------- Line Replaceable Unit
MOA------------------ Memorandum of Agreement
MOSA ---------------- Modular Open System Architecture
MPC ------------------ Most Probable Cost
MPLCC -------------- Most Probable Life Cycle Cost
NSA/NIAP----------- National Security Agency/National Information Assurance Partnership
NDA ------------------ Non-Disclosure Agreement
NDI-------------------- Non-Developmental Item
NDS ------------------ Non-Developmental Software
ORD ------------------ Operational Requirements Document
OS -------------------- Operating System
OSD ------------------ Office of the Secretary of Defense
OSI-------------------- Open Source Initiative
OSS ------------------ Open Source Software
OT&E----------------- Operational Test & Evaluation
OTD ------------------ Open Technology Development

PA---------------------- Process Area
PCA-------------------- Physical Configuration Audit
PDR ------------------- Preliminary Design Review
PDSS----------------- Post Deployment Software Support
PEO ------------------- Program Executive Officer
PLA -------------------- Programmable Logic Array
PLOC----------------- Probability Loss of Control
PM --------------------- Program Manager
PMD ------------------ Program Management Document
PO --------------------- Program Office
PRICE-S------------- Parametric Review of Information for Costing and Evaluation – Software
PSM ------------------- Practical Software & Systems Management
QC --------------------- Quality Control
RD -------------------- Requirements Development
REQM---------------- Requirements Management
RFP------------------- Request for Proposal
RMA ------------------- Reliability, Maintainability, and Availability
RR --------------------- Restricted Rights
RSKM---------------- Risk Management
S/SEE---------------- System/Software Engineering Environments
SAE------------------- Service Acquisition Executive
SAF-------------------- Secretary of the Air Force
SBIR------------------- Small Business Innovation Research
SCAMPI ------------- Standard CMMI Appraisal Method for Process Improvement
SCF------------------- Safety Critical Functions
SCN ------------------- Specification Change Notice
SD&D --------------- System Development and Demonstration or System Design and Development
SDD ------------------ Software Design Document or Software Design Description
SDF-------------------- Software Development Files
SDP------------------- Software Development Plan
SDR ------------------ Software Deficiency Reporting or System Design Review
SE---------------------- Systems Engineering
SEE------------------- Software Engineering Environment
SEER-SEM --------- System Evaluation and Estimation of Resource – Software Estimation Models
SEI -------------------- Software Engineering Institute
SEMA ---------------- Software Engineering Measurement and Analysis
SEP------------------- System Engineering Plan
SFR------------------- System Functional Review
SIL -------------------- System Integration Laboratories
SIS -------------------- Software Intensive Systems
SLOC----------------- Source Lines of Code
SMC ------------------ Space and Missile Systems Center
SNLR----------------- Specifically Negotiated License Rights
SOO ------------------ Statement of Objectives
SORAP -------------- Source of Repair Assignment Process
SOW----------------- Statement of Work
SPDP----------------- Software Professional Development Program
SPED----------------- Software Product Engineering Data

SPI -------------------- Software Protection Initiatives
SPM ------------------ System Program Manager
SPS-------------------- Software Product Specification
SQL------------------- Structured Query Language
SQT-------------------- Software Qualification Test
SRD ------------------ System Requirement Document
SRDR ---------------- Software Resources Data Reports
SRR ------------------ System Requirements Review
SRS------------------- Software Requirements Specification
SSDD ---------------- System/Subsystem Design Description
SSET ----------------- Source Selection Evaluation Team
SSP-------------------- System Safety Program
SSPP----------------- System Safety Program Plan
SSR-------------------- Software Specification Review
STINET -------------- Scientific and Technical Information Network
STSC----------------- Software Technology Support Center
SUM ------------------ Software Users Manual
SVR------------------- System Verification Review
SW -------------------- Software
SWA------------------ Software Assurance
TCP/IP --------------- Transmission Control Protocol/Internet Protocol
TD--------------------- Technical Data
TDP------------------- Technical Data Package
TEMP ---------------- Test and Evaluation Master Plan
TRD------------------- Technical Requirements Document
TRR------------------- Test Readiness Review
VDD ------------------ Version Description Document
UR -------------------- Unlimited Rights
U.S. ------------------- United States
USAF----------------- United States Air Force
WBS------------------ Work Breakdown Structure

J.3   Index